Praise for
One Word at a Time

"What is most astonishing about Dr. Linda Tessler's new book is her unique ability to have an intimate relationship with her readers, from introduction to epilogue. With wisdom and insight born of personal experience, she demystifies dyslexia's complexities and provides a structure for moving on. This courageous woman struggled with her own fears and anxieties, worked around the inadequacies of a non-supportive educational system, and found a path forward. If you are dyslexic, or if you are a parent, educator or someone who cares about a person wrestling with this potentially self-esteem-killing disability, you must experience this book – for your future's sake."

> — *John Kelly, President & Chief Executive Officer,*
> *Recording for the Blind & Dyslexic (RFB&D)*

"Dr. Tessler, herself a dyslexic reader, has written an immensely readable book that should be read by anyone interested in what dyslexia is and how it feels to have difficulty with reading or any other aspect of language, which includes speaking, writing, spelling, reading, and arithmetic. Specifically it should be read by parents, teachers, pediatricians, speech/language pathologists, and others who deal with dyslexic individuals. This "road map" shows you what dyslexia is, how it can be helped, how to cope with it, and how successful dyslexic individuals got to the top in their fields.

Read this book! If you can't read, listen to it on tape. Dr. Tessler tells you how."

> — *Sylvia O. Richardson, M.A.,M.D., Litt.D. (Hon.); Professor Emerita,*
> *University of South Florida; former President of the International*
> *Dyslexia Association and the American Speech & Hearing Association*

"Linda Tessler has given all of us parents of children with dyslexia a primer on personal motivation – as well as a substantial and useful resource guide. *One Word at a Time* is an engrossing journey of self-discovery that reminds us that while there are often no easy answers to developmental disabilities, self-limitations do not have to be part of the equation."

– Dennis M. O'Brien,
Speaker of the Pennsylvania House of Representatives

"Whether you are a layperson, a pediatrician, a psychologist, or anyone who wants to read one book to understand dyslexia, this is it. *One Word at a Time* is not only an excellent, thorough examination of dyslexia, but also a poignant, personal and very revealing look into how a sensitive and bright young girl faced living in a world of undefined and uncharted learning darkness. I almost feel ashamed of how easy life is for most of us, and how enjoyable it is to devour books without any serious thought of how difficult and overwhelming it must be for an intelligent person who can't easily, or perhaps not at all, read books."

– Sam McKeel, former editor-in-chief of the Philadelphia Inquirer

"Dr. Linda Tessler's new book, *One Word at a Time*, is a wise and thoughtful "road map" to guide all of us who are touched by the issue of learning disabilities. I especially related to her stories about her mother's unwavering support, as they highlight the vital importance of a mother's advocacy efforts in the life of her child. Dr. Tessler's book and her own life story are enlightening and inspirational to us all."

– Anne Ford, great granddaughter of Henry Ford;
Chairman Emeritus, National Center for Learning Disabilities;
*and author of **Laughing Allegra** and **On Their Own***

One Word at a Time

*A Road Map for
Navigating Through Dyslexia and
Other Learning Disabilities*

by

Linda G. Tessler, Ph.D.

One Word at a Time:
A Road Map for Navigating Through Dyslexia and Other Learning Disabilities

First Edition
Copyright© 2008 by Linda G. Tessler, Ph.D.

For further information, contact:
Dr. Linda G. Tessler at linda@onewordatatime.com

PHOTO CREDITS - istock
©Copyright www.istock.com:
Pg0 www.iStock.com/ blackred
Pg8 www.iStock.com/ArtisticCaptures
Pg12 www.iStock.com/Zocha_K
Pg20 www.iStock.com/Renphoto
Pg22 www.iStock.com/RonTech2000
Pg26 www.iStock.com/RichVintage
Pg32 www.iStock.com/marekuliasz
Pg37 www.iStock.com/peterspiro
Pg38 www.iStock.com/cydebergerac
Pg40 www.iStock.com/Palto
Pg42 www.iStock.com/duncan1890
Pg49 www.iStock.com/alengo
Pg54 www.iStock.com/pixelbrat
Pg58 www.iStock.com/Pitton
Pg64 www.iStock.com/MirekP
Pg72 www.iStock.com/Mateo_Pearson
Pg74 www.iStock.com/Eraxion
Pg78 www.iStock.com/Goldmund
Pg90 www.iStock.com/diane39
Pg92 www.iStock.com/nano

Pg102 www.iStock.com/EricHood
Pg113 www.iStock.com/GeofferyHolman
Pg114 www.iStock.com/Millanovic
Pg119 www.iStock.com/MarcusPhoto1
Pg120 www.iStock.com/DNY59
Pg125 www.iStock.com/digitalskillet
Pg126 www.iStock.com/Auris
Pg130 www.iStock.com/Terraxplorer
Pg138 www.iStock.com/johnwmiller
Pg140 www.iStock.com/hgmcgrath
Pg143 www.iStock.com/Viorika
Pg144 www.iStock.com/dystortia
Pg144 www.iStock.com/luoman
Pg152 www.iStock.com/imagedepotpro
Pg159 www.iStock.com/PinkTag
Pg164 www.iStock.com/hidesy
Pg168 www.iStock.com/pic4you
Pg170 www.iStock.com/alaincouillaud
Pg176 www.iStock.com/Zeffss1
Pg180 www.iStock.com/Andji
Pg189 www.iStock.com/phi2
Pg190 www.iStock.com/AskinTulayOver

Pg192 www.iStock.com/mstay
Pg214 www.iStock.com/ayzek
Pg217 www.iStock.com/jhorrocks
Pg218 www.iStock.com/theboone
Pg220 www.iStock.com/sjlocke
Pg226 www.iStock.com/JordiDelgado
Pg228 www.iStock.com/Mlenny
Pg234 www.iStock.com/matka_Wariatka
Pg238 www.iStock.com/Genericamerican0
Pg240 www.iStock.com/OliverChilds
Pg245 www.iStock.com/Sazonoff
Pg246 www.iStock.com/LuisPortugal
Pg258 www.iStock.com/civilman

PHOTO CREDITS - Tessler
©Copyright Linda Tessler: Pg31, Pg154, Pg160

PHOTO CREDITS - Carter
©Copyright 2000 Stephanie Carter
Illustration: Pg63, Pg84, Pg89, Pg129, Pg175, Pg186, Pg259

PHOTO CREDITS - Bill Beck Pg237

To my grandchildren born and unborn and to all our children:

May they find meaning in the struggles of their lives.

TABLE OF CONTENTS

Acknowledgments

It took a village. I could never adequately thank the enormous number of people who have made this book possible. I hope they know how deeply I appreciate them. May the good that comes out of this work serve as gratitude. We are passing it on.

Dennis J. Tessler is my husband, my lover, my family man, my friend and my wise advisor. We understand each other in the deepest way, where there are no words. I thank him for his steady presence over decades, for loving me through all my changes, and for believing in my work. His support means everything to me.

Frank Freudberg (www.freudberg.com) helped me with the actual writing of this book. He is a journalist, writer, corporate communications consultant and a remarkable professional with whom to work. Frank's skill and patience enabled me to find my written voice. He gave of his talents and time far beyond what was expected of him.

So, too, did Robert Tessler, M.D. Although he is my brother-in-law, Rob feels more like a brother. He unselfishly and modestly shared his expertise, no matter how much time it took, enabling me to find my professional voice. Retired from Family Practice, Rob lives in Boca Raton, Florida, with his wife, Jill, who has been a dear friend – more like my "big sister" – through the years.

Joyce Eisenberg (www.thewordmavens.com), my talented editor, polished this pearl – my book. I admire her facility with words, both their nuance and their spelling. I appreciate her patience and excitement in being part of this project and her recognizing that the account of my personal journey was as important as my professional advice.

Although these editors say that each word and thought was my own, I know they did very "heavy editing" to translate the work from Linda-ese into English.

When it came to wading through Web sites about publishing, my poor reading became a problem again. Thankfully, Jay Carter, Psy.D. (www.jaycarter.net) talked me through the publishing process and helped me figure out how to get this book into print.

Sara Hodgson (www.incompra.com), an artist and graphic designer, immediately had a sense of what the landscape of this book should look like. She transformed the manuscript into an attractive and accessible book.

I could not have written this book without the loving support of family members and friends. I was born to one of the most wonderful mothers, Nancy Avery Silovitz Greenbaum. My father, Marvin Greenbaum, never stopped trying and always loved me. I have the fondest of memories of my grandparents, Julia Shapiro Silovitz, Charles Silovitz, and Reba Zehugut Greenbaum, and of my sister, Barbara Ellen Zelt, who is also a cherished friend. When I met Denny, my family expanded to embrace his. His mother, Mildred Tessler, read to me for my licensing exam and still spontaneously reads signs to me at museums. The community of caring people extends to Denny's sister, Cindy Auslander; her husband, Sam Auslander; and their daughter Becky, who has volunteered her expertise in promoting this book. I also appreciate my cousins, nieces, nephews, aunts and uncles on both sides, like Aunt Libby and Uncle Al.

My sons have grown into fine men and married equally fine women. I'm grateful to Keith for his willingness to let me include his story in this book. His courage in the face of his own dyslexia inspired me. I appreciate his wife, Marjorie, for her continued interest and willingness to read the manuscript. I'm thankful for Brian, who keeps me laughing and joins me in the joys of my life. Even when he was in high school, Brian would hang out with me. He joined me at yoga and ballroom dancing classes; together we've traveled to China and taken flying lessons. I'm thankful, too, for his wife, Erin, who has brought so much love and thoughtfulness to our clan. They all understand the meaning of family.

My friends are like family to me. I've known Marlene Solomon for 40 years. She and Saul, now her husband, went to the prom with Denny and me. One afternoon when we were lounging in her hammock, Marlene read *The Velveteen Rabbit* to me. She later read to me for my licensing exam, and she read this manuscript in a not-very-pretty early draft.

The thought of leaving somebody out of the acknowledgments
takes me back to my childhood, when my mother gave me
a special stuffed animal to sleep with. I was worried that
my other animals would be sad if they didn't
get to sleep with me, too, so I put them all in my bed —
and there was almost no room for me!

Linda Levin came to my house to help me remove the clutter from my desk, so I could keep up while writing the book. Sandra Jacobs used her hyperlexia (extremely good reading skills) to help me choose an author. And how could I have gotten through this without the love and counsel of Shelly Eisenberg? Everyone should have a friend with as much free-flowing love. The deepest appreciation to other friends, past and present, who also excel at listening and loving; among them are Lynne Solomon, Ruthie Rosenfeld, Linda Gloss, Dara Burger, Paul

Brewington, Marsha Birnbaum, Phyllis (Green) Gross, and Rita Landsman and Jessie Korn, my college roommates.

Dorothy and Clyde Shives, Noriko Lovasz, Dominic Rapino, Debbie Michalik and Patricia O'Brien have not only stayed with me throughout this long process but have also done excellent and conscientious work.

Harriet May Savitz (www.harrietmaysavitz.com), an award-winning writer, has believed in this project for 30 years. She would not let me forget about doing it. Plus, she inspired me by having written 24 books. Her books for children with disabilities have broken down attitudinal barriers and popularized wheelchair sports.

Janet Hoopes, Ph.D., Milton Brutton, Ph.D., and Larry Kaiden knew me from the very beginning of my professional work. These three mentors, who are now all deceased, believed in the contribution I could make. Their encouragement meant so much.

Sally Shaywitz, M.D., neuroscientist and author, has done groundbreaking research on dyslexia; one of the reasons I wrote *One Word at a Time* was to share her findings with a wider audience. Charna Axelrod, Ed.D., reviewed the sections of the book that focused on neuropsychology. Nancy Hennessey lent her expertise about the resources available to dyslexic readers. Joy Lesser edited the original article about the Six Clues to Successfully Managing a Learning Disability, which appeared in a professional journal.

When I was 32, I went to the Orton Dyslexia Conference (now the International Dyslexia Conference) in Washington, D.C. There were days of workshops and thousands of people, and I was overwhelmed. I told a woman about my problem and asked her how I could find out about dyslexia. In response, she ushered me to a table piled with the

Annals of Dyslexia. I asked if they were on tape. They were not. I still recall my tears of frustration. Afterward, I wrote to every board member of the Orton Dyslexia Association to see if these books could be put on tape. Sylvia Richardson, M.D., wrote back and offered to do whatever she could to help. Sylvia is remarkable woman – sensitive and powerful.

I've been privileged to know Sylvia Richardson, Mel Levine, M.D., and Ed Hallowell, M.D., along with the late Sally Smith, Margaret Rawson and Roger Saunders, from my attendance at meetings of the International Dyslexia Association. They have mentored me without knowing they were doing so. I'm grateful, too, to those at the Philadelphia Branch of the IDA, who have welcomed and supported me.

Thanks to the staff of Recording for the Blind & Dyslexic, particularly to Jodi Button, past executive director of the Philadelphia Branch, who volunteered to read this book for the CD recording, and to Peter Smith, the retired national Senior Vice President of RFB&D Learning Through Listening, who added his expertise to this manuscript in its final version. I'm indebted to John Kelly, national President and CEO. Because of John's support and his commitment to recording and distributing this book on CD, I know it will be read – or listened to. I'm proud to call him my friend. On behalf of all dyslexic readers, I want to let RFB&D volunteers know that they change the lives of their listeners.

The International Dyslexia Association, Recording for the Blind, and I were all born the same year. It seems that our time had come.

Out of the kindness of his heart, Henry Winkler, a dyslexic reader, granted me an interview many, many years ago. He was busy being the Fonz on *Happy Days*, but he took time to call me anyway. His trust and endorsement of this book mean so much to me personally. Thank you, Henry.

Thanks, also, to the eight other famous and successful people who graciously took time out of their busy lives to talk candidly with me – a lowly doctoral candidate. They are Harvey Fierstein, Sen. Mike Gravel, Bruce Jenner, Jackie Stewart, Lindsay Wagner, Charles Drake, Ph.D., Arthur Ochs Sulzberger, and the late Dr. Richard Wyatt. Their experience with dyslexia formed the basis for my dissertation and then fueled this book.

During the year I was home alone writing this book, I would take a break to watch *Oprah* every afternoon. Coincidentally, she was doing a series entitled "Dreaming Your Wildest Dreams." I used her program as motivation to stay in action and to continue to write *One Word at a Time*.

This book owes its existence to all those who have assisted in its creation and those who have been kind enough to love and encourage me to be me.

Thank you.

Preface

A Clue

I was a little girl in first grade in a Philadelphia public school. My teacher asked me to carry a note to Mrs. Vonzaghetti, whose classroom was down the hall.

Because this was the first week of school, my teacher wanted to be certain I knew where I was going. She asked me to repeat the teacher's name. I didn't hesitate. I proudly said the name I had heard.

"Mrs. Spaghetti."

My teacher's face went blank. She repeated it several times for me, but I still couldn't get it. I just couldn't do it.

Because of the way my dyslexic brain works, I was unable to distinguish the difference between Vonzaghetti and spaghetti. I didn't know this at the time. I wouldn't understand it until many years later.

...

It has taken me almost 50 years to be able to share my experience with dyslexia: a three-decades-long struggle and the challenges, realizations, failures and successes I had along the way.

In this book, I've interwoven my personal story with my professional perspective. At age 32, my word fluency and accuracy tested on a third-grade level, yet I earned a Ph.D. and became a clinical psychologist specializing in learning disabilities. I'm also the parent of a son with dyslexia. From this vantage point, I offer you this road map to travel from where you are to where you want to be. The book is enriched with inspiring stories that I gathered for my dissertation, when I interviewed prominent people who succeeded despite their learning disability.

Writing this book was a painstaking process because of my own dyslexia. It is imperfect, but it is honest. This is who I am. There is nothing special about me. I can't take a lot of credit. I've been surrounded by wonderful people – family and friends. I've followed my path and my passion and did what was deeply satisfying to me. And I took advantage of the opportunities that were available.

My motivation is to help you avoid some of the struggles that I and countless others have experienced. While I've used my experience with dyslexia as a starting point, these insights and guidelines apply to other learning disabilities as well.

Who This Book Is For

For anyone who wants to know how to practically and psychologically manage a learning disability: It should be the first book people read when they discover that they, their children, or loved ones have a learning disability, which affects between 15 and 20 percent of the population.

For dyslexic readers: Whether or not reading is difficult for you, this book is for you. Get through it one word, one page or one chapter at a time. Or, listen to a recorded version.

Parents who are spending so much of their time and money to remediate a child will find guidance here. They can learn how to raise a resilient child rather than one who is victimized by his learning disability.

Teachers who want to understand the emotional realities of students with learning disabilities – and how to help them with the resulting psychological issues – should read this book, particularly the chapters about my struggles in school, the tips for reading recorded text, and the Six Clues to Successfully Managing a Learning Disability.

Professionals, including psychologists, pediatricians, social workers and speech pathologists, who want to be able to pick up just one book to get a better understanding of a learning disability and its emotional ramifications will find that resource here, along with tips on how to guide others through this journey.

Those of us with learning disabilities walk a perilous tightrope. Either we will fall and become victims of our learning problem or we will develop strength, resilience and competence by taking this journey.

This book is a guide for that journey. It is not a nuts and bolts book about what school to place your child in, where to get tutoring, and what programs are best. For that information, you'll need to look elsewhere.

Millions have gone on this journey before me, and even more will take it after me because of what is now available. One of them should be you or your loved one.

What prevents people with learning disabilities from reaching their potential is simply being unaware of what's known about the field and what resources are available. This book is about spreading the knowledge that is available – and offering ideas about how to use it.

Introduction

A Users' Manual

My goal is to get you started on the road to a deeply satisfying life by helping you deal with a learning difference. To succeed, it's up to you to meet the challenge.

What research has revealed about dyslexia – that it is a neurologically based processing problem – will probably hold true for other learning disabilities as well. Likewise, the strategies and tips I offer will be useful for anyone with a learning difference.

This book has been written to match the way those with dyslexia read. Some sections are more work to read than others. I need you to hang in there with me. The ideas are important, and I have taken poetic license with complex research to make it understandable.

Terminology

One of the most common learning differences is dyslexia, a language-based learning disability. Children with dyslexia have trouble learning to read. Once they learn, the process usually remains slow and laborious. Spelling is difficult. Remembering proper nouns is challenging. Learning a foreign language is problematic. Frequently, speech development is slow. A high percentage of children with dyslexia also have Attention Deficit Disorder or Attention Deficit Hyperactivity Disorder.

Other learning disabilities have different sets of characteristics that impact development and achievement. These might include a short attention span, difficulty following directions, eye/hand coordination problems, a poor memory, or trouble adjusting to change.

"Learning disability," the legal term used by educators and professionals, allows someone to be diagnosed and to receive treatment. I prefer the term "learning difference," because I know that we all can learn — we just do it differently. An easy way around this is to use the abbreviation "LD." I predict that in the future, the term "learning disability" will be out of fashion. Instead, we'll analyze how children process information and teach them accordingly.

Till then, what we need most is information. What prevents people with learning disabilities from reaching their potential is simply being unaware of what's known about the field and what resources are available. This book is about spreading the knowledge that is available – and offering ideas about how to use it.

---

*The way you view a problem either creates a solution
or deepens the problem.*

We, as a society, cannot afford to have people fall short of their potential. There is work to be done. Education, knowledge and commitment to the axiom "Be the best you can be" are the most powerful weapons.

This book will inform you about:

The nature of dyslexia and other learning disabilities and how medical science can explain what you are experiencing. It is physiological, not psychological.

- Six life strategies – or clues – that you can incorporate into your life or use to assist a loved one in overcoming learning difficulties.

• A list of what not to do. *(See Chapter 16: "Do Not Enter Zones.")*

• Accommodation techniques for learning differences.

• How to avoid the trouble spots when raising a child
with a learning difference.

• What it's like to have a learning disability:
You are not alone, you are in good company,
and you don't have to reinvent the wheel.

A Powerful Technique for Dyslexic Readers

If your reading is not what you would like it to be, try this:

Contact Recording for the Blind & Dyslexic (www.rfbd.org, 800-221-4792) for a recorded version of this book. You can sign up directly if you have a documented learning disability, or get it through your school, if the school is a member. You can also purchase the CD where you bought the book or download it from the Internet.

Listen to the recording and follow along in this text. This often increases your interest and understanding of the material, while helping you see how new words look in print. With this process, your reading can improve. Don't try this new technique at just one sitting. Listening is a skill that gets better with practice.

All readers should try the following:

Do something with what you are learning. Teach yourself in a multi-sensory way. Use all three sensory modalities – seeing, hearing and doing (what professionals call kinesthetics). Underline, highlight and make notes about the main ideas and proper nouns you encounter.

Create a picture in your mind or draw charts of the concepts. This reinforcement helps the memorization process, and that's essential.

If as you read, you incorporate some of these ideas into your life, then you will be doing important, life-changing work. If the things you want to integrate seem overwhelming, then pick just one or two. I challenge you to incorporate even one idea from this book into your life. It will make a huge impact. This is an incredibly simple concept – yet it is incredibly powerful. Please try it.

Most important of all, **trust yourself**. Individuals with learning difficulties usually have a lot of well-intentioned people giving them both useful information and misinformation. Believe what your gut tells you, and use outside resources as needed.

Those of us who struggle with reading will not be able to read as many books as a good reader does. But that's not so bad when you think about it: You just have to choose your books very carefully. I'm confident that if you make a commitment to read this book one section, one page, or even one word at a time, you'll look back and be glad you did.

What You Need to Pack For Your Trip

❏ A working understanding of your learning disability.
    See "Road Work Ahead," Chapters 5-7 and seek out
    other sources.

❏ Your emotional intelligence. Don't worry: you can pick up a
    lot more along the way.
    See "Thinking, Feeling and Dealing," Chapters 8-10.

❏ A healthy dose of curiosity and self-motivation.
    See "Finding Motivation," Chapter 23.

❏ Strategies for dealing with the challenges presented by
    your learning difference and for achieving your life's goals.
    See "Mapping Out a Road to Success," Chapters 27-28.

❏ The ideas in this book that inspire you to take action.
    Refer to the notes you make on pages 18-19.

I WANT TO APPLY THESE IDEAS TO MY LIFE

This book is a guide. When you read about an idea that gives you that "aha" feeling, use the space below to make notes about anything you want to try or just remember. Dog-ear the page so you can find it quickly later on.

_____

_____

_____

_____

_____

_____

_____

_____

_____

_____

_____

_____

_____

_____

Before I Knew
I Needed to Go
on a Trip

"*Since I was the stupidest kid in my class, it never occurred to me to try and be perfect, so I've always been happy as a writer just to entertain myself. That's an easier place to start. Always look on the bright side of things. Be positive; negativity is the mother of failure. If you believe in yourself, you will somehow succeed.*"

- Stephen J. Cannell, dyslexic reader, novelist and Emmy Award-winning writer/producer, whose television shows include *The Rockford Files, Hunter* and *21 Jump Street*.

CHAPTER 1

OVER THE RIVER AND THROUGH THE WOODS

Over the River and Through the Woods

It was a snowy morning in 1957, the week before Thanksgiving. I was 8 years old, a third-grader in a Philadelphia school.

Something bad was about to happen.

Earlier that morning, Mrs. Rhodes, my teacher, had announced that the Messenger of the Day would be me – Linda Greenbaum. There was nothing more exciting.

Messengers were allowed to leave the classroom once or twice – more if they were lucky – to take envelopes to other teachers and notes to the principal's office, to get the janitor if something spilled, and even to escort kids to the nurse. It was great. Every child lived for this day.

Around 10:30, just after math, as the other students were putting away their books, I received my first assignment.

"Linda," Mrs. Rhodes called out. "I need my Messenger of the Day! Please come up." I skipped to the front of the classroom. The other kids were jealous.

Although Mrs. Rhodes was addressing me, she spoke so the whole class could hear. "Linda, this is an important message." She handed me an envelope. "Can you tell me where it goes?"

I held the envelope in my hand. There were letters written on it, but I didn't know what they said. I stared at them. I felt my face flush. To steady myself, I leaned against the blackboard. I still remember the cold fear that rushed through me.

I had a secret that I was good at keeping. No one knew it. No one. Even Mrs. Rhodes hadn't quite figured it out yet.

My secret was that, for some reason, I couldn't read. Despite everyone's help – teachers, parents, and grandparents – I just didn't catch on. I thought I was stupid. I managed by memorizing things and repeating them. When people thought I was reading from the blackboard, I wasn't. I was remembering.

"Linda," Mrs. Rhodes said gently. "Come on now. You can't deliver the message if you don't know where it goes." The kids were beginning to murmur.

Mrs. Rhodes shifted her weight from one foot to the other. "Linda! Where-is-this-envelope-supposed-to-go?" She stabbed her finger at the printing. "Come on ... that's a word we had in spelling just last week!"

I knew the first word. I didn't read it. I just recognized it.

"The – ." I stared at the letters of the other word. They made no sense. I could see the letters but I couldn't put them together. I knew that the first letter was "O" but I couldn't figure out how an "O" sounds. And I couldn't put the other letters together to even make a guess.

"The what?" There was no warmth in Mrs. Rhodes' voice. No appreciation that I knew the word "the." The kids began snickering and enjoying my discomfort. My face turned red.

"The what ... Linda? *The what? The what?*"

I stared. Those letters wouldn't register in my brain. Even at age 8, I knew that something was very wrong. And now, I was being shamed by the only person I thought would be able to help me – Mrs. Rhodes.

I couldn't just stand there. I looked at the envelope again. "The ... the ... gym ...?" I said.

"The gym?" Mrs. Rhodes said. "No, not the gym! The office. The office! O-F-F-I-C-E!"

My classmates burst out into laughter. Mrs. Rhodes quieted them down, but it didn't matter. I remember trying not to cry.

"Well, it seems this is not a good day for Linda to be our messenger," Mrs. Rhodes announced. "So, who else would like a chance?"

The classroom exploded into a chorus of kids shouting, "Me! Me! Me!" They waved their hands and stretched their arms. They were excited and jumping up and down, and that was fine. It took their attention off of me. I slithered back to my desk, trembling and holding back the tears.

A little later, when we were dismissed for lunch, I went to the girl's room, locked myself in a stall and sobbed quietly, trying to muffle the sound with my hands.

That was a long, frightening day, and although I didn't realize it then, it was the beginning of a private struggle that would last another three decades.

CHAPTER 2

MY CHILD ON BOARD

My Child on Board:

Keith's Turn

Fast-forward 24 years. My first son, Keith, was in third grade, the same grade I was in when my struggle was exposed. He was bright and happy and had tons of friends.

I packed his lunch and sent him off to his school. Later that morning he called me from a pay phone at school. "Mom," he said, "something's wrong. I can't do my work. I need help."

Those words chilled me! I'll never forget them. He was devastated and brave at the same time. I knew that whatever Keith's problem was, getting him the help he needed would become the most important thing in the world for me.

At the time, he was attending a private school where he was learning Hebrew as well as English. It was driving him crazy.

Ancient languages, developed before the discovery of paper and designed to be carved in stone, are read from right to left. English, of course, is read from left to right. That began with the advent of the pen, so the writer would not smear the ink with his hand.

There was a good chance that Keith's problem was dyslexia. Trying to learn those two languages simultaneously would be impossible for him.

As quickly as possible, my husband, Denny, and I made an appointment with Dr. Milton Brutton, a psychologist who specialized in administering psychoeducational evaluations. He gave Keith a complete battery of tests.

When the results came back, we went to see Dr. Brutton. He informed us that our son was a dyslexic reader. A shiver went through my body. Just a few months earlier, I had been diagnosed with dyslexia, but I didn't fully understand what it meant. Actually, nobody knew much about dyslexia in 1981, but I knew I didn't want this for my son. What parent would?

As the news sank in, I stood up, slid the chair back under the table, and walked to a far corner of the room. As I turned to the wall, tears streamed down my face. I fought to muffle the sobs. The pain was sharp. I was sick to my stomach that my oldest son would have to go through the same struggles I went through. I wanted to make the reality go away.

A Different Approach

While doing research for my dissertation on famous people who had overcome dyslexia, I interviewed Dr. Richard Wyatt, a psychiatrist, neurologist and a world-renowned brain researcher. He mentioned that he had just found out that one of his children had dyslexia. "What a shame," I said. "You don't get it," he replied. "I believe that one of the reasons I've been able to discover things my very intelligent colleagues couldn't find is because of my dyslexia. I look at things from another perspective. I think I've done so well as a researcher because I approach and solve problems differently."

I tried to maintain decorum, but it was useless. I felt as if I were alone in the bathroom stall again, not wanting anyone to hear me, trying to hold back the tears.

Frequently, when children are diagnosed with a learning disability, their parents discover that they, too, have been coping with a similar problem their entire lives. "Oh, I do that, too," they might say. Or, "That's just like me." Learning disabilities run in families.

Denny and Dr. Brutton, apparently at a loss, just sat there. For a long couple of minutes no one moved. I pulled myself together, returned to the table and, with a few tears still rolling, seated myself. I was ready to get to work to help my son.

Denny and I set out to do everything possible to help Keith: to support him, to provide appropriate tutoring so he could learn to read, and to place him in a good educational situation. But even in the best of situations, with supportive parents and a good system, dyslexia still hurts. That is one of the most upsetting realities.

We decided to immediately take Keith out of his private school and enroll him in a smaller school designed to meet his particular academic needs. This was a financial burden for our family, but the real concern was that Keith would be amputated from the wonderful social and cultural environment he had enjoyed over the past three years. That's tough for adults and excruciating for kids.

At his new school, Keith got involved with computers from the start. He could understand their workings. He had an ability to visualize interactive systems and could put things together without reading the instructions. Many times, he was asked to help the headmaster solve his own computer problems. He thrived academically, but he was hampered socially. There were not many students in his new class.

Although I didn't know it at the time, Keith would soon adjust. His social sphere would revolve around his friends in our neighborhood.

…

Today, despite significant dyslexia, Keith is a tremendously successful businessman. He holds a civil engineering degree from Lehigh University and an MBA from Villanova University. He is Chief Operating Officer (COO) of a business that is flourishing, the only company of its kind. He single-handedly invented a unique infrastructure that permits the company to enjoy unprecedented growth and profitability. Keith's ability to creatively solve problems, organize, think outside of the box and apply advanced technology is a key to the company's success.

My son is a much better reader than I am, although he prefers to learn by listening to books rather than reading them. He is an "avid listener." His spelling, the most difficult of the language processes to remediate, is still poor.

Even with all the accommodations Keith has made, his dyslexia is still very much alive and well. Although he is a computer professional, he has banned himself from online chat rooms because his spelling is so poor that others in the room think he is a child.

Not long ago, Keith sent an e-mail to hundreds of employees and contractors that read, in part, "Please accept my apology for the incontinence." (Incontinence means "the inability to retain urine," which is not the same as inconvenience, the word he meant to use.) I've defined these words for my fellow dyslexic readers, because I know I would have trouble with them, too.

Keith, Dennis and Brian Tessler

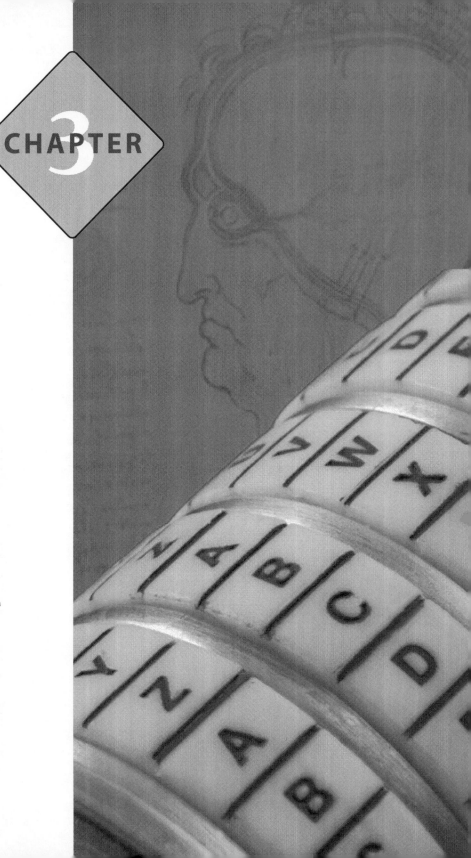

EINSTEIN, DA VINCI AND YOU

Einstein, da Vinci and You

What was it that my son and I were facing? What was this thing they call dyslexia? It's no wonder we were all confused. I was, and maybe you are, too. The professionals – including experts in schools of education at world-class universities – contradict each other on such basic issues as whether or not dyslexia even exists.

The Dyslexia Debate

On the day of the oral examination for my doctoral dissertation, I was informed that Temple University's Reading Department was refusing to let my dissertation go through. I had researched the characteristics and coping strategies of nine famous people with dyslexia. The Reading Department faculty didn't recognize "dyslexia" as a legitimate term. "It's a garbage term," they said.

The professors on my Dissertation Committee, most of who were from the Psychology Department, were stunned. They apologized. This was quite unusual. The orals are usually just ceremonial; rarely do candidates get delayed because of them.

I was given the go-ahead when I agreed to label each subject as a "self-perceived" dyslexic. What's ironic is that I had already been officially diagnosed with dyslexia by a psychologist who specialized in learning disabilities. But he was on the faculty of another university, where dyslexia was not a "garbage term." It would be years before there was agreement that dyslexia was real.

Dyslexia does exist. It is neurological in origin. With the development of magnetic resonance imaging (MRI), we now know more about which parts of the brain are being used when an individual is reading. We also know that because their brains are "wired" differently, dyslexic readers have more trouble translating written images into words than "good" readers do.

Most people don't realize that reading – unlike speaking, running and laughing – doesn't come naturally. It has to be consciously learned, like riding a bike or making soup. Dyslexia can cause problems with reading comprehension and vocabulary development. We have hard evidence that people with dyslexia simply take longer to process the written word, which makes learning more challenging. People with dyslexia also read less, which reduces their general knowledge.

Dyslexic readers vary as much among each other as they do from the general population. And dyslexia comes in an incredible array of flavors, shapes and sizes, distinguished by the variety and severity of the specific weaknesses that are involved.

It's sad to think that in the past, children with dyslexia were labeled retarded or emotionally disturbed. It was commonly thought that their language problems were caused by an emotional block. They were lumped in with kids who were physically challenged or who had behavioral problems. The only thing they had in common was that they were uncommon.

Dyslexic brains are not inferior to the brains of people who read on grade level, although they are certainly different.

If you have dyslexia, you are in good company. So many people with dyslexia are above average in intelligence that it's mind-boggling.

Every single one of them had or has a real struggle with reading and has taken this journey.

Think about Albert Einstein's scientific accomplishments. He was a theoretical physicist and a Nobel Prize winner. Experts believe he had dyslexia.

Dyslexia creates reading problems, not impairment of thinking, failure of imagination or deficiency of courage. Great poets, statesmen, artists and others, like William Butler Yeats, Winston Churchill, Gen. George Patton, Leonardo da Vinci, Pablo Picasso and financier Charles Schwab, traveled the road you're on, too.

Dyslexia is not an excuse. It is an explanation.

— Anonymous

When you are at the movies or watching television, think about Jay Leno, Robin Williams or Whoopi Goldberg. They've been on this path, and so has heartthrob Patrick Dempsey of *Grey's Anatomy*. He spent 12 years in special education classes. Early in her career, British actress Keira Knightley struggled with learning her lines, but by working tirelessly with her mother and some teachers, she found success: She went on to star in *Pride & Prejudice* and the *Pirates of the Caribbean* series.

Going shopping for some clothes? American fashion designer Dana Buchman has taken her daughter on this trip.

It was rumored that King Carl XVI Gustaf of Sweden had dyslexia. Journalists reported that he misspelled his name when signing his accession document and again when he wrote his name on the wall of a copper mine. In 1997, he admitted it publicly when his wife, Queen Silvia, addressed the issue.

Driving around downtown? Henry Ford encountered the same detours and potholes you face.

When you discover that someone you know has dyslexia, it's almost always a surprise. There doesn't seem to be anything wrong with that person, and in a very real sense, there isn't.

Hans Christian Andersen is a Danish author and poet who had dyslexia. No one could read his manuscripts, but I'll tell you this: Tens of millions of people read his stories.

It's understandable that in our literate culture, those who are not able to read are stigmatized, which often sets the stage for significant emotional and behavioral problems. To teachers, employers, friends and family, dyslexic readers often seem to lack motivation or to be easily frustrated.

Yes, they get frustrated, but it is inaccurate to say "easily." Persistence and discipline are important skills – often acquired with great difficulty – and are key to whatever success dyslexic readers enjoy. Ask Thomas Edison, famous for ceaselessly trying a thousand different materials until he finally found the right one and invented the light bulb!

Dyslexia creates reading problems, not impairment of thinking, failure of imagination or deficiency of courage.

THE OYSTER DOES IT, TOO

The Oyster Does It, Too

One night a long time ago, I went to my desk to find a form that I needed. When I took off the necklace that my husband, Denny, had given to me, its small, round, perfect pearl became dislodged from the setting. I heard it drop. It must have been somewhere on the desk, but I couldn't find it. I searched for two solid hours. I was so upset, I couldn't even tell Denny, much less ask him to help me look. I could not stop looking for it. I couldn't get it out of my mind.

That missing pearl taught me a lesson, which I'll get to later in the story. But for now, the pearl is a suitable metaphor.

Do you know why certain oysters produce pearls, while other oysters wind up on someone's plate in a seafood restaurant?

The oyster that produces the gem did so to protect its internal organs from a foreign substance (often sand) that made its way into its shell. The oyster reacts to this irritant by beginning a slow, steady process of coating the irritant with microscopic layers of nacre, a substance that eventually becomes a pearl.

The oyster survives, and the world gains a gem.

The point is obvious. With the appropriate reaction, something destructive or debilitating can often be molded into something valuable.

Keep reading to see how a learning disability – yours, your child's, your spouse's, your friend's, or your co-worker's – can evolve into something of exquisite value.

Road Work Ahead

"The greatest stumbling block preventing a dyslexic child from realizing his potential and following his dreams is the widespread ignorance about the nature of dyslexia."

– Sally Shaywitz, M.D., neuroscientist and author of *Overcoming Dyslexia: A New and Complete Science-Based Program for Reading Problems at Any Level*

HOW DYSLEXIA REVEALS ITSELF

I need your patience now. This is a must-read section. It is technical, but it will help you better understand learning disabilities.

How Dyslexia Reveals Itself

Dyslexia = Difficulty Processing Language

"Dyslexia" – coined from Latin – is defined as "word blindness." Dr. Pringle Morgan first described it in 1896 in a paper that appeared in the *British Medical Journal*.

Dyslexia was "discovered" by medical doctors, who are in the business of recognizing symptoms. And in their eyes, patients with dyslexia were figuratively blind to words. But there is a lot more to it than that.

Dyslexia is a common, widespread learning disability that interferes with the development of language skills and, most troublingly, with reading skills. Simply stated, dyslexic readers have difficulty processing language.

- *Dyslexia is not necessarily letter or word reversal.*

- *Dyslexia is not a disorder you can outgrow.*

- *Dyslexia is not an indicator of laziness or low intelligence.*

- *Dyslexia is not mirror writing.*

It is important to note that dyslexia occurs in otherwise normal, healthy, and motivated children – despite the facts that their vision and hearing are intact and that they are getting an appropriate education.

Actor and producer Henry Winkler, alias "The Fonz" in the TV series **Happy Days**, *admitted that because his father told him to always count change, he would pretend to do so. In fact, he couldn't actually count it.*

Dyslexia exists on a continuum. Some people have it worse than others.The symptoms and signs of dyslexia are unmistakable, yet dyslexic readers are frequently misdiagnosed or not diagnosed at all. The more intelligent an individual, the less likely he or she is to be diagnosed.

Indications of Dyslexia

The most common indications of dyslexia, according to the International Dyslexia Association (www.interdys.org), include problems in the following areas:

- learning to speak
- organizing written and spoken language
- learning letters and their sounds
- memorizing number facts
- spelling
- reading
- learning a foreign language
- doing math operations correctly.

In Preschool Children:

Signs of dyslexia in preschool children include talking later than expected, a slowness to add new words to their vocabulary, difficulty rhyming, and trouble following multistep directions.

The signs of dyslexia include:

- difficulty reading single words, such as a word on a flashcard
- difficulty learning the connection between letters and sounds
- confusing small words, such as *at* and *to*
- letter reversals, such as *d* for *b*
- word reversals, such as *tip* for *pit*.

Having one of these signs does not mean a child has dyslexia; many children reverse letters before the age of 7. But if several signs exist and reading problems persist, or if you have a family history of dyslexia, have your child evaluated.

Dyslexia affects more boys than girls. True or false?

FALSE: *While boys tend to act out and be referred for educational testing, girls more often keep quiet and hide out. That's why boys are diagnosed with dyslexia three times more often than girls. But if all the children in the class were screened, the boy/girl ratio would be fairly equal.*

In Younger Students:

As children are emerged in classroom learning, additional problems sometimes show up.

Does Your 1st, 2nd or 3rd-Grader:

- remember simple sequences such as counting to 20, naming the days of the week, or reciting the alphabet?

- have an understanding of rhyming words, such as knowing that fat rhymes with cat?

- recognize words that begin with the same sound (for example, that bird, baby, and big all start with b)?

- easily clap hands to the rhythm of a song?

- frequently use specific words to name objects rather than using words like "stuff" and "that thing"?

- easily remember spoken directions?

- remember names of places and people?

- show understanding of right/left, up/down, front/back?

- sit still for a reasonable period of time?

- make and keep friends easily?

Answering "no" to some or most of these questions may indicate that a child has a learning disability, although not all students who have difficulties with these skills have dyslexia. Formal testing is the only way to confirm a diagnosis of suspected dyslexia.

In Adolescents and Adults:

The following difficulties are often associated with dyslexia if they are unexpected for the individual's age, educational level, or cognitive abilities:

- reading problems

- poor spelling; relying on others to correct spelling

- poor handwriting

- working well below one's intellectual capacity in a job

- difficulty with planning, organization and management of time, materials and tasks.

On the other hand, adults with dyslexia:

- may have an excellent memory (which they rely on)

- often have good "people" skills

- often are spatially talented; many choose to work as engineers, architects, designers, artists and craftspeople, mathematicians, physicists, physicians (esp. surgeons and orthopedists), and dentists.

- may be very good at "reading" people (intuitive)

- frequently excel as entrepreneurs.

A qualified diagnostician can test a person to determine if he or she is truly dyslexic.

The Dyslexic Entrepreneur

What's the connection between entrepreneurs and dyslexia? According to Julie Logan, a professor of entrepreneurship at the Cass Business School in London, dyslexics are drawn to entrepreneurship because "the strategies they have used since childhood to offset their weaknesses in written communication and organizational ability — identifying trustworthy people and handing over major responsibilities to them — can be applied to businesses."

What's staggering are the numbers. According to Logan's 2007 survey, 35 percent of the U.S. entrepreneurs she interviewed identified themselves as dyslexic. To succeed, they've used their excellent communication and problem-solving skills and their ability to delegate authority.

"If you tell your friends and acquaintances that you plan to start a business, you'll hear over and over, 'It won't work. It can't be done.' But dyslexics are extraordinarily creative about maneuvering their way around problems," she says.

Successful business leaders with dyslexia include Richard Branson, founder of Virgin Atlantic Airways; Charles Schwab, founder of the discount brokerage firm that bears his name; and Paul Orfalea, founder of the Kinko's chain of stores, which provide copying and printing services.

Some Problems at the Heart of Dyslexia

Researchers are continually developing a deeper understanding of the complexities of dyslexia, but for now, we'll explore some of the fundamental problems that create language difficulty.

What are the specific weaknesses that impact reading?

[Double Deficit Hypothesis - (Wolf, Bowers: 1993)]

* **Phoneme Awareness**

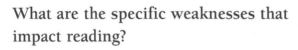

* **Rapid Naming**

See spot run.

Phoneme (sound) awareness is the ability to hear the differences between sounds. Dyslexic readers have problems with this, particularly in hearing the distinctions between the sounds that make up a word, especially the vowels.

Remember what happened when I was asked to take a note to Mrs. Vonzaghetti, the other first grade teacher in my school? I couldn't hear the difference between her name and the word "spaghetti" – even though my hearing was normal. I would also have trouble distinguishing between *nozzle* and *nostril*, for example.

Not surprisingly, people with poor phoneme awareness confront the same challenge when dealing with a foreign language. If we were given a phrase in Spanish, for example, we would have difficulty reproducing the sounds.

Rapid naming is simply the ability to name something quickly.

When you read a word, you must be able to say each sound quickly. For example, the sounds *bi kin i* make no sense separately, but together they form the word *bikini*. Likewise, for a sentence to have meaning, the words must be read in rapid succession. The phrase, "The dog is playing with his stuffed animal" means little when you say each individual word, but it makes sense when you say the words one right after the other. The inability to name sounds quickly and automatically can make subsequent learning difficult.

Those with rapid naming problems may also have trouble reciting the multiplication tables quickly.

Reversals: Many, but not all, dyslexic readers tend to reverse words and letters, such as *b* and *p*, *d* and *g*, or *g* and *q*. Sometimes people with dyslexia may go right when they are told to go left. Reversals are not used as a diagnosis for dyslexia; in fact, we expect young children to reverse words and letters when they are learning to read.

Information on demand: While a dyslexic reader may have a problem bringing back information on demand, he or she may not have difficulty when the information is used spontaneously. For example, if you wanted to tell a friend about a restaurant where you dined last night, you would have no problem doing so. But if that friend asked, "What is the name of that restaurant?" you might have trouble recalling it. When asked, you might also have trouble recalling the names of the actors in a movie you saw last night, or maybe even the name of the movie itself.

Dyslexia may be the result of one or more of the above problems or other weaknesses. Children with just one problem will have difficulties learning to read but may catch up in a later grade. Those with more than one problem may not be able to compensate and may never catch up to their peers.

The Trauma of Reading Out Loud

No matter how much progress we make in reading, reading out loud usually causes us to stall.

- My mother had dyslexia and didn't know it. Years ago, when someone would ask her to read out loud, she would pretend she didn't have her glasses.

- Bruce Jenner, who won the gold medal in the Decathlon at the 1976 Olympics, told me that he was comfortable going out and meeting the world on the athletic field. But reading out loud? That would never happen. He makes it perfectly clear: "I will not read out loud. Period." Jenner went on to become a commentator for ABC and NBC television.

• When he first auditioned for acting roles, Harvey Fierstein failed because of his lack of confidence and poor ability to read aloud the works of others. He overcame this by writing his own Tony Award-winning plays – *Torch Song Trilogy* and *La Cage aux Folles*.

• When he was a child, former *New York Times* publisher Arthur Ochs Sulzberger was called to the front of the auditorium to read something to the entire school. He became so distraught that he broke out in massive hives and could not perform. The next time he was scheduled to read aloud, he took the precaution of taking antihistamines, which had the unexpected effect of putting him soundly to sleep.

• Henry Winkler said that when going to an audition, he had trouble reading the script. He would take it into a bathroom stall and try to cram the words into his brain.

Religious rituals often create a lot of trouble for people with dyslexia. Ceremonies and services are loaded with reading aloud "opportunities."

Then there was me. I remember this clearly: One day in sixth grade, when I returned to my classroom after lunch, I saw that the teacher had rearranged the desks into a giant circle. We were going to spend the afternoon reading a social studies book *out loud*. I'm not sure, but I think that triggered my first-ever anxiety attack.

As we began reading, I counted the number of students who would read before it was my turn. I tried to predict which sentence would be mine, and I read and re-read it. I invented other avoidance techniques, too, which I would rely on for the next 20 years. I ducked down to tie my shoes. I needed to sharpen my pencil. I suddenly had to go to the bathroom.

I was running out of tricks. It was getting closer and closer to my turn to read, and I wasn't feeling so good. My heart was pounding out of my chest, I was clammy and feverish, and I felt lightheaded. This time, it was no charade. I really had to leave and get myself to the nurse's office.

By the end of the day, I had gotten away with reading only one sentence aloud. After we all had one turn, my classmates began to volunteer to read. My teacher never called on me, although she did call on other kids who didn't raise their hands. I don't think that was an accident. The teacher must have caught on.

Although people with dyslexia can improve their reading skills – sometimes dramatically – reading out loud remains problematic. There's no way to avoid revealing that you have a problem with language.

The audience does not respond well when an individual with dyslexia – even a playwright, an actor or the publisher of *The New York Times* – reads aloud. The slow, awkward cadence isn't easy on the ears.

And for the readers? Even though they may have achieved success as adults, the challenge brings them back full circle to their school days and reminds them how much they dreaded reading aloud.

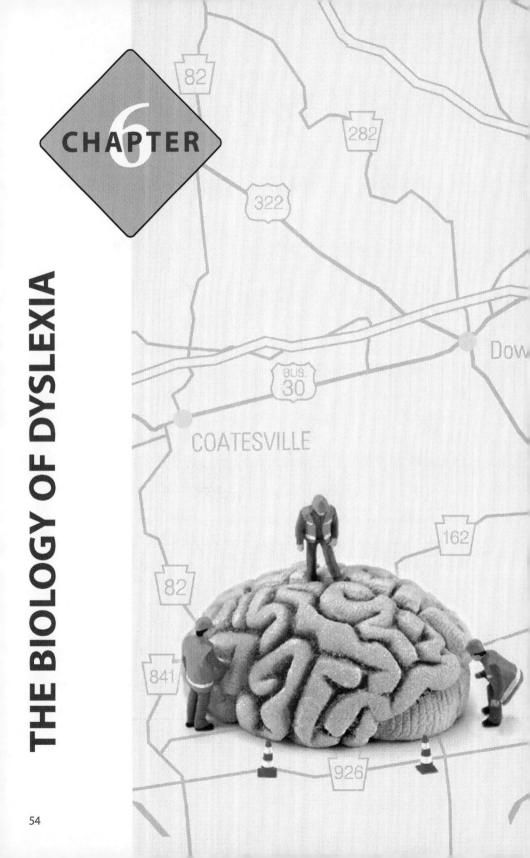

CHAPTER

6

THE BIOLOGY OF DYSLEXIA

The Biology of Dyslexia:
Same Destination, Different Route

I like to simplify the biology of dyslexia like this: Good readers take the highway to town, while dyslexic readers take the back roads. These roads are nerve pathways that connect the different areas of our brain, and they are very, very busy when we are reading.

Language is processed on the left side of the brain in the following three areas:

1. Broca's area, in the inferior frontal gyrus *(in front and low in the brain),* is involved with beginning reading, such as sounding out words.

2. The parietotemporal area *(near the middle of the brain and relatively near the top)* is concerned with analyzing the meanings of words.

3. The occipitotemporal area *(in the back and low behind the ear)* manages the appearance of words as if they were pictures and immediately associates them with their sound and meaning.

These words are then linked with information coming from other parts of brain; associated with their sounds, pictures and meanings; and stored.

You don't need to remember the parts of the brain; you just need to understand the concept. In plain terms, the dyslexic reader is reading primarily with the front of the brain, while the "normal" reader is reading with the back of the brain.

The "Normal" Reader's Brain: The better the reader, the more easily can he or she bypass the first two areas – the sounding out and analyzing operations – and go directly to the third area. In fact, the higher the reading score, the more activation we observe in the occipitotemporal area on an MRI (#3 on the diagram below).

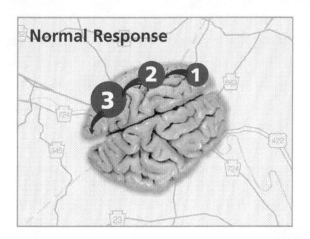

The Dyslexic Reader's Brain: A dyslexic brain does not use its occipitotemporal area as efficiently as does a "normal" brain. Instead, it tries to compensate by relying more on the Broca area's sounding-out abilities. On an MRI, the Broca's area, the center of speech production, is observed as being overactive (#1).

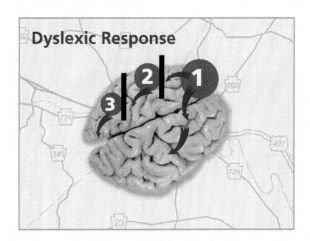

As a result, dyslexic readers have difficulty associating word forms with the sounds and meanings of language. Interestingly, many sub-vocalize (move their lips) when they read. I do this, and it helps, especially when I am reading difficult material.

There are certain dyslexics whose brain "wiring"
appears to be the same as in good readers,
but due to poor teaching or lack of exposure to reading,
their pathways are underdeveloped.

Physical evidence explains why dyslexic readers process information more slowly and why reading may be tiring. It's no surprise that many dyslexic readers report brain fatigue.

These different brain-use pathways generally don't change or improve with time. However, preliminary studies are revealing that with intense remediation, it may be possible to improve the brain wiring in adults. Dyslexic readers can compensate by calling into play other areas in the right side of the brain, but they will not read as efficiently as a "good" reader does.

There is absolutely nothing diseased or damaged about the brain of someone with dyslexia. It simply selects a different pathway when processing language, just as we are right-handed or left-handed. We all have brains that are more competent at certain tasks than others. This is the human experience.

Evolution of the Brain

If we look at the evolution of the brain, it's easier to understand why so many of us have difficulty reading. We have been using speech for half a million years longer than we've been reading.

In fact, the human brain has not developed a region dedicated to reading, as it has for other abilities, such as speech. Humans left on their own will speak, but they will not read. It's fair to say that the part of the brain we use for reading is moonlighting, because it was designed for something else.

Before the invention of the printing press, dyslexia was not a disability, but when the written word gained importance, people mistakenly equated the ability to read with intelligence. Today, psychologists

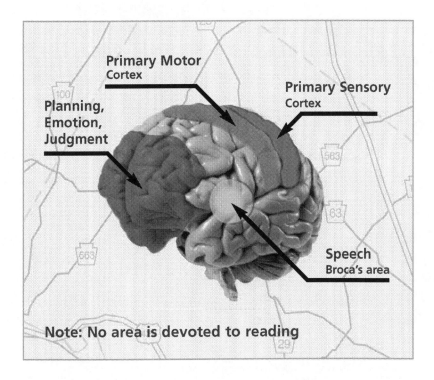

Primary Motor Cortex

Primary Sensory Cortex

Planning, Emotion, Judgment

Speech Broca's area

Note: No area is devoted to reading

have adopted a more expansive understanding of intelligence. There is social intelligence, emotional intelligence, musical intelligence, and more – not just academic intelligence.

Some of the abilities found in those with dyslexia, such as critical thinking, creative problem solving and resourcefulness, may have even been an advantage when we were cave dwellers. We didn't die off in the process of natural selection.

The Importance of Early Intervention

With early exposure to an intensive reading program, children with dyslexia can become much better readers. There is also evidence that with specific kinds of intensive training, brain pathways can be "rewired," so their reading conduits are more like those of normal readers.

Reading programs take different approaches, so before you select one, it's important for a reading teacher to pinpoint the reading problem – whether it's with sight words, decoding or comprehension – in order to make a good match.

It's important to understand that fluency, defined as the ability to read a text accurately and quickly, is hard to remediate. People with dyslexia generally learn to accept the fact that they read more slowly than others. It's generally not a problem, unless they are asked to read aloud.

Another option is to hire a specially trained teacher who has participated in an accredited training program. When trying a new reading program or hiring a tutor, it's best to have a trial period after which time you can evaluate the success of the program. If you don't see any improvement, try something else.

There is much you can do at home as well. Expose kids at risk to language games like Pig Latin. Read Dr. Seuss aloud, because the rhythm of the words and the word play are helpful. Play rhyming games. Talk to your children about science, tell them how things work, and engage them in high levels of reasoning, which is where the dyslexic reader usually excels.

Montessori schools teach in a multisensory way. All kinds of intelligences and styles of learning are nurtured: musical, kinesthetic, spatial, interpersonal, intrapersonal, intuitive, and the traditional reading, writing, and math. The majority of their programs are for children ages 3 to 6, although there are also infant/toddler programs.

For more information, see Child on Board: Directions for Parenting, chapters 29-31.

Finding the Help You Need

Following are some well-respected programs. This is not a complete list; you may come across other good programs. In addition, research is continuing and new programs are being developed.

READING PROGRAMS

You can access multiple resources for information about reading programs.

The International Dyslexia Association (www.interdys.org) publishes a Matrix of Multisensory Language Programs, which describes several programs, such as these:

- The phonics-based **Wilson Language Training** (Phone: 800-899-8454, www.wilsonlanguage.com), which is particularly helpful for those with decoding difficulties, is used in many schools throughout the country. Barbara Wilson did a superb job of incorporating many of the principles of the Orton-Gillingham approach into a more user-friendly program.

- **Lindamood-Bell Learning Processes** (Phone: 800-233-1819, www.lindamoodbell.com) is an effective "jump-start" program that strives to bring a child's reading pretty close to grade level. This short-term intensive instruction has dramatically changed the lives of the many children who have had the privilege of participating.

- **Language Circle/Project Read** (Phone: 800-450-0343, www.projectread.com) trains teachers; its alternative curriculum is also used in some schools. The program offers language arts instruction in three areas: encoding/decoding, reading comprehension and written expression.

IMSLEC (The International Multisensory Structured Language Education Council, www.imslec.org) accredits training programs that emphasize the use of visual, auditory and kinesthetic-tactile methods to help students learn to read and spell, rather than focusing on a sight-word (memory) method, tracing method or phonetic method alone.

TEACHERS AND TUTORS

The following organizations certify teachers in particular methods:

- **The Academic Language Therapy Association** (ALTA; www.altaread.org) certifies individuals in the delivery of academic language therapy, which develops effective secondary language and written communication skills through proficiency in reading and writing.

- **The Academy of Orton-Gillingham Practitioners and Educators** (AOGPE; www.ortonacademy.org) certifies individuals in the Orton-Gillingham approach, which teaches students about language structure using multisensory, structured, sequential, cumulative and cognitive methods.

- **Wilson Language Training** certifies individuals in the Wilson Reading System.

COMPUTER PROGRAMS

- The **Edmark Learning System** (Phone: 888-640-1999, www.enablemart.com/Edmark-Reading-Program-Software) sells award-winning reading software and hardware, such as the Readingpen, an assistive reading device for school-age reading levels. Its Reading Program software teaches beginning reading and language development to nonreaders and those who have been unsuccessful using other programs.

Believe it is possible to solve your problem.
Tremendous things happen to the believer.
So believe the answer will come. It will.
- Norman Vincent Peale

UNDERSTANDING YOUR LEARNING DIFFERENCE

Understanding Your Learning Difference

Dyscalculia
Dyslexia
Dysgraphia
Attention Deficit Disorder
Non-Verbal Language Disability
Expressive Language Disorder

By understanding dyslexia, we can begin to understand other learning disabilities. Because dyslexia was one of the first learning disabilities to be identified, we understand it better than the others. What we know about dyslexia's physical nature is probably an indication of what we will discover about other learning processes, such as dysgraphia (problems with the physical act of writing) and Attention Deficit Disorder.

Learning disabilities are neurologically based processing problems with a diverse set of characteristics that affect development and achievement. Some of the symptoms can be found in all children at some time during their development. However, children with learning disabilities have a cluster of these symptoms (probably the result of brain wiring), which do not disappear as they grow older. With accommodation and training, these symptoms may become less intense or bothersome.

Symptoms of Learning Disabilities

The Learning Disabilities Association of America (LDA) has identified the following symptoms; the indications of dyslexia are included among them.

Put a check in the box next to the symptoms that apply to you or your child:

Most frequently displayed symptoms:

❏ short attention span

❏ poor memory

❏ difficulty following directions

❏ inability to discriminate between/among letters, numbers or sounds

❏ poor reading and/or writing ability

❏ eye-hand coordination problems; poor coordination

❏ difficulty with sequencing

❏ disorganization and other sensory difficulties

Other characteristics that may be present:

❏ performs differently from day to day

❏ responds inappropriately in many instances

❏ distractible, restless, impulsive

❏ says one thing and means another

❏ doesn't adjust well to change

❏ difficulty listening and remembering

❏ difficulty telling time and knowing right from left

❏ difficulty sounding out words

❏ reverses letters

❏ places letters and words in incorrect sequence

❏ difficulty understanding words or concepts

❏ delayed speech development; immature speech

❏ difficult to discipline

Learning Disabilities Association of America, 2004

What Is A Processing Problem, Anyway?

A learning disability is identified by the specific weakness or weaknesses that are involved. The problems show up in any one or more of the four stages of learning: input, integration, memory and output.

Continue to think about which of the following issues apply to you. All of this information is useful in understanding your learning disability. It is not a complete description but it will get you started.

COMPONENTS OF LEARNING

A. *Input:* mostly visual, auditory and kinesthetic perception

B. *Integration:* sequencing, abstraction, and organization

C. *Memory:* working memory, short-term memory,
and long-term memory

D. *Output:* speaking, writing, drawing, and gesturing

*This information was outlined in an article in LDA Newsbriefs
(2004), a newsletter published by the Learning Disabilities Association
of America (www.ldanatl.org, 4156 Library Road, Pittsburgh, PA
15234; 412-341-1515). I recommend that you join this organization;
as a member, you'll receive the newsletter.*

A. INPUT

First, we need to get information *into* our brains. This is referred to as "input." Think of it this way: Information comes in through one of our five senses: sight, hearing, touch, smell or taste. It also comes in through "kinesthetics" – when we learn by doing.

The majority of information is brought into the brain through the eyes (visual perception) or through the ears (auditory perception).

Visual perception problems make it difficult to recognize subtle differences in shapes. For example, it may be hard to distinguish a person from the ground on which he is standing. If your depth perception is poor, you may bump into things. If you have poor eye-hand coordination or "visual-motor" trouble, you might have difficulty hitting or catching a ball. You might rotate or reverse letters or numbers, such as *d* and *b*, *p* and *q*, or *6* and *9*.

Auditory perception problems make it difficult to distinguish subtle differences in sounds or to separate the sound you are listening to from the background noise. You may also have trouble differentiating between similar sounding words, such as *kite* and *bite*, *sip* and *sill*, *bet* and *but*.

An individual may have a problem with visual perception or auditory perception, or both.

The more senses you use to process the information,
the more likely you will be to absorb it and utilize it.

B. INTEGRATION

After information is put into the brain, it needs to be integrated, which means we mix it together with what's already in our brain – background data. This includes:

Sequencing: Information must be put into the right order. A person with sequencing problems might mix up the order of the months of the year.

Abstraction: The information needs to be understood beyond its literal meaning. This is where we form concepts by inferring ideas from the information we are given. Someone who has problems with abstract thinking might have trouble understanding the meaning of concepts and might not understand jokes or word puns.

Organization: Information needs to be arranged into complete thoughts or concepts. Someone with difficulties in this area might have trouble being on time, organizing the facts collected for a term paper, or keeping a desk uncluttered. He or she may frequently forget or lose things.

C. MEMORY

Information then needs to be retained. These three types of memory are important for learning:

Working memory means holding on to information until the parts are blended into a complete thought or concept. This allows us to read each word in a sentence and remember it until the end of the sentence, so we can understand the content.

Short-term memory means storing and retaining information for a short period of time. We might be able to remember the topic long enough to do well on a test, or remember the name of someone we meet at a party long enough to introduce him to somebody else.

Long-term memory means storing information so that it is available over a long period of time. To do this, we need to review the information again and again so it becomes a lasting part of our knowledge.

D. OUTPUT

Finally, for information to be useful, it needs to be communicated. This is usually through words or movement, such as writing, drawing or gesturing.

Language output can be "spontaneous" – when we initiate a conversation and have the chance to organize our thoughts before speaking – or "on demand," when we are asked a question and are expected to respond. Spontaneous conversation is easier than on-demand conversation.

Someone with a learning disability usually takes longer to organize his thoughts and find the right words. Often, our listeners get impatient: Conversation has a rhythm and people expect us to keep pace with them.

Those with a motor, or movement, disability might have trouble with fine motor skills, such as coloring, cutting and handwriting. Or, they may have trouble with gross motor skills, such as jumping and running.

...

We need to demystify our learning difference by understanding it, says Dr. Mel Levine, author of numerous books including *Keeping Ahead in School: A Student's Book About Learning Abilities and Learning Disorders*. Levine, a pediatrician and expert in developmental behavior, explains that a diagnosis is not necessarily the most important part of what we discover, unless the diagnosis will provide services. But we do need to understand our limitations and strengths.

Thinking, Feeling, and Dealing

"I have developed what I believe to be my dyslexia-enhanced skills in three-dimensional space perception and eye-hand coordination by becoming an ultrasound expert. I truly feel that my difficulty in reading and spelling is a small price to pay for these natural gifts in other areas."

– Beryl Benacerraf, M.D., Professor and Researcher, Harvard Medical School

CHAPTER 8

EQ is a greater predictor
of success than IQ.

BOOSTING YOUR
EMOTION INTELLIGENCE

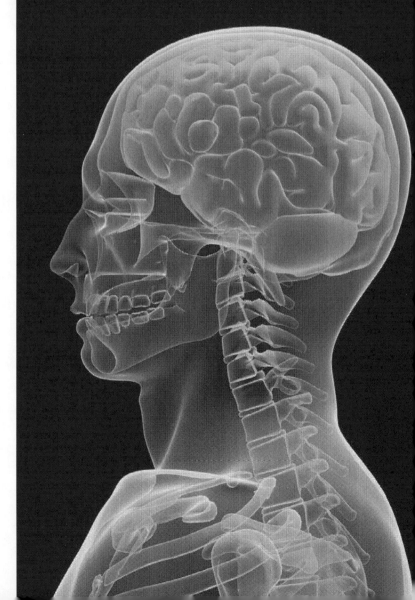

Boosting Your Emotional Intelligence

Emotional intelligence (EQ), a concept developed by Howard Gardner, a psychologist, educator and professor at Harvard University, suggests that there's much more to intelligence than IQ. His Theory of Multiple Intelligences challenges the notion that there is a single indicator of human intelligence. He believes that our view of what makes someone smart is very incomplete, because it fails to take into consideration an array of essential skills and talents that are major factors in the degree of success we achieve.

The concept of emotional intelligence is just beginning to be taught in some schools. EQ includes the following elements:

- self-motivation

- persistence in times of difficulty

- delaying gratification

- self-control

- self-management

- ability to empathize

- rapport

- self-soothing

- passion that's well directed

- taking calculated risks

- knowing one's feelings and being able to manage them

- knowing one's thoughts and being able to manage them

- knowing one's feelings about one's thoughts

- reading the thoughts and feelings of others.

Emotional intelligence doesn't mean you have to be nice all the time. It means knowing how to confront others when necessary and how to walk a tightrope when you need to.

Just as everyone has strengths and weaknesses, we also have strengths and weaknesses in our emotional intelligence. For example, we may be good at empathizing but not very good at managing our feelings.

In times of trouble, someone with emotional intelligence can, metaphorically, climb a hill and gaze down at himself with a better perspective. He can clearly identity his thoughts and feelings about the situation and see the best game plan. He can understand the thoughts and feelings of others – and then make appropriate choices about his own behavior.

Of course, no one can react this way all of the time. The trick is to do it most of the time.

Persistence in times of difficulty, one aspect of emotional intelligence, is particularly valuable in modern times. World-renowned brain researcher Richard Wyatt, a dyslexic reader who was schooled at Harvard, observed that the "golden boys" – the extremely bright students who had lived their lives being the smartest in their classes – often cracked under the academic pressure of the Ivy League. Everything had always come easily to them. They had no real experience dealing with adversity or getting back on the road. They were neither resilient nor adaptable.

When I first interviewed Tony Award-winning actor and playwright Harvey Fierstein for my dissertation, he told me that he had tried to learn to drive a car. He would reverse the gas and the brakes, so he gave up. Years later, he called to tell me that he had finally learned to drive — and he was very proud of himself. He did it by gutting it out, by persevering. He had literally gotten back on the road.

The key to a successful journey is to pack all the emotional intelligence you have. Don't worry about not having a particular item. There will be countless opportunities to pick up more along the way. In fact, the difficulties in life are opportunities to develop more emotional intelligence, and a learning disability gives us many such chances.

No one develops character while coasting. It happens as a result of our struggles. The vicissitudes of life help us develop the heart we need to persist and succeed at the goals we set for ourselves.

That's emotional intelligence.

CHAPTER 9

HOW THEY SURVIVED
AND THRIVED

Success ↗

How They Survived and Thrived:

Advice From Famous People With Dyslexia

For my doctoral dissertation, I interviewed nine celebrities who identified themselves as having dyslexia. Although the details of their lives varied, the broad outline was the same: After years of struggling in school, they each found a talent or passion that they nurtured. They used the lessons learned from dealing with dyslexia, such as the necessity for self-motivation, perseverance and resourcefulness, on their road to success. They all had a healthy dose of emotional intelligence.

…

When he was struggling with the work in elementary school, **Harvey Fierstein's** parents gave him glasses, and the teacher moved him nearer to the blackboard. It didn't help his dyslexia. He says he became a clown, developing his personality and focusing on what he did well. He made light of his problems.

As a teen, Fierstein read plays instead of books, because they had a lot fewer words. Today, he's an award-winning playwright and actor. He urges dyslexic readers to take advantage of all the help that's available. Although it might be difficult and boring, in the end it's wonderful to be able to read a book. "Everyone's mind works differently. Don't be embarrassed, he says."

…

Mike Gravel, the former Democratic U.S. Senator from Alaska (1969-1981) who declared his candidacy for president in 2006, considers having a learning problem as not much different than being blond-haired, blue-eyed or short. "It's what you're born with. I wasn't born to look the way I thought I should look. I thought I should look like Gregory Peck. So you live with that," he says. "Play the cards you are dealt with. Make them an asset. Too many people get bogged down wishing they had different cards."

"The development of wisdom is more important than the accumulation of knowledge."

– Mike Gravel

...

Olympic gold medalist Bruce Jenner, who had to repeat second grade, reported developing an enormous drive to excel in athletics to overcome his feelings of inadequacy in the classroom. As an athlete, he got the recognition and pat on the back he craved.

Jenner told his mother that he won the decathlon because of the emotional lessons dyslexia had taught him – tremendous determination and an ability to deal with pressure and failure. "It was 80 percent a mental challenge and 20 percent a physical challenge," he says. He tells children this: "Find something you're good at and do it. That will build your confidence."

...

Race car driver Jackie Stewart grew up in Scotland, "feeling dumb, humiliated and basically unhappy." Although he dropped out of school at age 15, he was determined to become good at something. He went to work in his father's garage, where he discovered that he was good at practical things, such as servicing cars.

He went on to become one of the finest racing car drivers in history, winning more Grand Prix races than any other driver. From his dyslexia, he developed a pattern of compulsive hard work and scrupulous attention to detail. A perfectionist, he is extremely organized and allows himself no errors, which served him well in race car driving. "God gives everyone a gift of some kind," he says. "It's a question of identifying that gift. But identifying it isn't enough. Develop it, manicure it, polish it."

...

On television, **actress Lindsay Wagner** played the Bionic Woman, a tennis player who was nearly killed in a skydiving accident. After she was surgically rebuilt, she had amplified hearing, a super strong right arm, and legs that enabled her to run faster than a speeding car – a super woman, of sorts. This was a far cry from Wagner's childhood, during which she was "embarrassed, horrified, frustrated and out of control" because of her dyslexia and the impending divorce of her parents.

She found her way by immersing herself in the fantasy world of acting, at which she excelled.

Her advice? "Forget what the world thinks you should be. Forget the standards others set for you. Look at yourself and see what you're good at and see what turns you on, what inspires you. Then start growing in that direction. You're responsible to make yourself happy and to find a place for yourself."

...

Actor, producer and author Henry Winkler created his character — The Fonz in the TV series *Happy Days* — to project everything he wished he had been in high school: self-reliant, self-respecting and personally confident. He recalls his actual school experience: "If I couldn't do well in the subject at least I could make people laugh, which is something that would allow me to shine."

To parents, he says, "Ten good minutes of just listening to whatever your child has to say is worth a lifetime. Being listened to and listening is one of the most important and respectful acts a human being can do for another human being."

...

Educator Charles Drake, Ph.D., was voted the worst speller in his forth grade class and could get through Latin only by cheating. Years later, he earned a doctorate in education from Harvard and was a Fulbright Scholar in Denmark. In 1970, this educator and licensed psychologist founded the Landmark School for students with language-based learning disabilities. In 1984, he founded Landmark College in Vermont, the nation's first college for students with dyslexia.

Dr. Drake says his occupation is a direct result of his learning problems. Because of his own linguistic difficulties, he was motivated to help dyslexic children. He believes that children with good intelligence can be taught language as a "scientific inquiry, like programming a small computer." He suggests that English should be taught as a science, and spelling rules should be learned. To children, he says, "Ask for help, use everything you have and work hard. Don't use dyslexia as an excuse."

...

The late **Dr. Richard Wyatt, a brain researcher**, advised children to concentrate on the future, rather than the present.

"You could repeat several grades in elementary school and still become a doctor later on because nobody cares what you did in elementary school," said Dr. Wyatt. This expert in the functioning of the brain believed that "basically, none of us are meant to read and write. It is artificial."

His early experience with dyslexia taught him to be a problem solver and made him familiar with the challenges and frustrations of doing scientific research. "If I can't do it one way, I'll find a different way. I can solve problems in unique ways," he said.

...

"Advice?" I have enough trouble giving my own children advice," laughs **Arthur Ochs Sulzberger, former publisher of *The New York Times*.** He does advise children to expose themselves to different activities so they can gain a new perspective in regard to their abilities. He reports that this happened to him in the Army, where he was surprised to learn that he was capable and intelligent. He also advises parents, who he believes are much more alert (to learning problems) than parents were in his youth, to get the help that's presently available.

Sulzberger's accomplishments provide an example of someone who did what he could to change his world and the world around him. When he was at the helm of *The New York Times*, he insisted on simplicity in the writing. He attributes this emphasis to his own experience with dyslexia. "I firmly believe that the best writing is the simplest kind of writing."

MAKING YOUR DEFINITION ROAD-WORTHY

Making Your Definition Road-Worthy

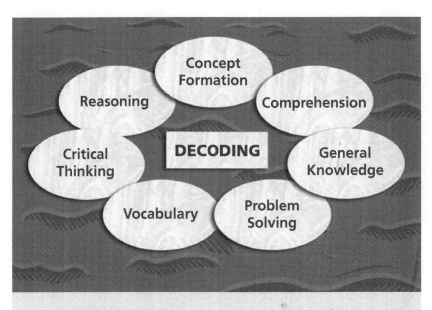

"In dyslexia, an encapsulated weakness is surrounded by many strengths." - Dr. Sally Shaywitz, in *Overcoming Dyslexia: A New and Complete Science-Based Program for Reading Problems at Any Level*

The way we see a particular situation can create a problem or solve it. If we see it only in terms of our limitations, then there is a problem. But if we see dyslexia like Sally Shaywitz does – as "an island of weakness in a sea of strengths" – then our thought process empowers us rather than limits us.

I believe that Dr. Shaywitz's definition is on the mark, as evidenced by the tremendous contributions dyslexic readers have made to the world over the centuries.

Our differences have advantages and disadvantages. Often, dyslexics are multidimensional thinkers, visually oriented and imaginative. They can be creative, inventive and determined. They stand out as hands-on learners. Research has indicated that many dyslexics are gifted in perceiving spatial relationships. Who knows what else scientists, researchers or educators will discover about dyslexia and dyslexic readers?

Researcher Norman Geschwind observed that efforts to prevent dyslexia may be wrongheaded, because in many people the disadvantages of dyslexia may be directly linked with the advantages. In other words, in trying to prevent dyslexia, we may be throwing the baby out with the bath water.

In his book *In the Mind's Eye*, Thomas West writes that successful dyslexic individuals may have achieved greatness not despite their dyslexia, but as a direct result of it. Because people with dyslexia are so in touch with their nonverbal, visual-spatial intelligence (the right-hemisphere modes of thought), they have trouble with orderly, sequential verbal-mathematical tasks. West says that the complex traits referred to as "learning disabilities" and "dyslexia" may be, in part, the outward manifestation of a different way of thinking.

The Good News

Dyslexics are overrepresented among top-ranking artists, scientists, and business executives. What are the possible advantages of this difference?

Dyslexic readers may:

- *think outside of the box*

- *learn in unconventional ways*

- *develop perseverance*

- *hone their ability to deal with adversity*

- *have significant strengths in reasoning, problem-solving, concept formation, critical thinking and perceptions of spatial relationships.*

If you want the world to see your learning difference as a weakness among strengths, then you must first see it that way yourself. If you want the world to see you as capable, then you must see yourself as capable of utilizing your strengths and managing your weaknesses. How we define a learning disability in our own minds is pivotal to our success or failure.

Listen to yourself carefully. What do you tell yourself about your learning difference?

Your mind has evolved over eons to *answer any question posed to it.*

Let's say you make a big mistake. If you ask, "Why am I such a damned idiot?" you will get an answer about your personal flaws. But if you ask, "How can I avoid making that mistake again?" you will get a completely different – and a totally more important – answer.

Never, ever, ask yourself the wrong question.

It's important to test your definition of your learning disability to see if it limits or empowers you. So, for example, if your definition is negative and limiting, you use phrases like:

- "There's nothing I can do about it."

- "That's just the way I am."

- "They make me so mad."

- "They won't allow that."

- "I have to do that."

- "I can't."

- "I must."

- "If only."

If your definition is positive and empowering, you use phrases like:

- "Let's look at our alternatives."

- "Can I choose a different approach?"

- "I control my own feelings."

- "I can create an effective presence."

• "I will choose an appropriate response."

• "I choose."

• "I prefer."

• "I will."

Those of us with a learning disability travel a perilous road. Either we will become victims of our learning differences, or we can take the experience and strengthen ourselves by learning basic life lessons.

The skills needed to overcome a learning disability are essentially identical to the skills everyone needs to get to where they want to be.

 These are the keys to success for *all* people in *all* situations. And these principles are not new — they are as old as mankind.

The Trouble With School

"I was, on the whole, considerably discouraged by my school days. It was not pleasant to feel oneself so completely outclassed and left behind at the beginning of the race."

Sir Winston Churchill, Prime Minister of the United Kingdom (1940-1945 and 1951-1955). A dyslexic reader who failed eighth grade, Churchill went on to be a prolific author: he won the Nobel Prize in Literature in 1953 for his historical writings.

CHAPTER
11

THE BEGINNING OF
MY JOURNEY

The Beginning of My Journey

I was the firstborn child of loving parents. They believed that education was important. After World War II, my father worked his way through school on the GI Bill. My mother was wonderfully attentive and read to me every night.

My mom was ahead of her time. She was an amateur psychologist dedicated to being the best mother possible. She was determined to see that her children had self-esteem and felt competent in their abilities to take care of themselves.

Women of her generation were expected to be supporters of their husband's lives – not wholly developed themselves. She wanted more than that for her daughters. She wanted us to be able to support ourselves and earn a living if ever we needed to. She wanted us to have the competency she never achieved for herself.

Elementary School

As a little girl, I was all excited about going to school. I remember the first day of first grade, laying out my clothes, getting my notebook and pencil case ready.

My mom walked me to school, and I couldn't wait for the day when I was big enough to walk by myself. There were "safeties" along the way, and that looked like a cool job. The good students were the ones picked to be safeties. I told myself I wanted to become a safety.

Once I settled into my new surroundings, I began to see that life in first grade wasn't going to be exactly as I had expected.

I remember sitting at my desk as the teacher held up a sign with the word "red" on it. "This is the word red," she said. (She was using the sight recognition method to teach reading.) I thought this was the greatest thing in the world. *I can read it.* "Red!" I was on my way.

At least that's what I thought.

I was eager to learn to read, especially because my mom had read to me so much. But learning to read by sight words is not the best approach for the way my brain functions. At the time, teachers did not use phonetics – which deals with the sounds that make up words – to teach reading. That would have probably been a better approach for my learning style.

---

*When my sister, Barbie, began to learn to read, it bothered me.
She was four years younger than me, and she was picking it up fast.
Why was she learning to read when I hadn't learned yet?
I was jealous.*

The truth is, I was usually in a fog or blackout when it came to words. Words never were – or never would be (as I'd someday learn) – easy for me.

No matter how hard I tried or how carefully I did my homework, I kept being placed further and further back in the reading groups. I couldn't figure out how the other classmates were getting it while I wasn't.

Small Acts With Big Impacts

Throughout my life, from childhood until today, I've had a lot of important help from the people around me.

This help has made a huge difference. At first, while I was still in hiding, I tried to go it alone. That was a mistake. It's vital for someone who is struggling with learning to be able to ask for and accept help from others. Timing is everything. If you learn to ask for help *before* things fall apart, you save yourself, and plenty of other people, a lot of grief and frustration.

...

I had tremendous trouble learning right from left. But my mother came to the rescue. She bought me a ring to wear on my right hand. They both begin with the letter "R," I thought. *Ring means right, right means ring. Ring means right, right means ring.* It worked. I still remember the feeling of that ring on my hand. Ring means right, right means ring.

...

My Grandpop Charlie, a man grounded in reality, recognized that something was wrong with my school performance. He saw that I was trying and trying and not really making progress. He somehow figured out that my problem was with words and language, not with thinking.

He told me, "Honey, if you sit quietly in your chair at school and just pay attention, you will learn enough to at least pass. You're the kind of kid who understands more than people realize. You are smart in your own kind of way."

My Mom-Mom Julie used to say, "You know, sometimes you are not too smart and you are not dumb either." That truth was refreshing: I am not smart sometimes. But I knew how much she loved and believed in me. I decided to adopt Mom-Mom and Grandpop's survival strategy: Sit there. Be patient. Pay attention. It was simple. And for a long time, it worked.

. . .

Then there was the nightmare of the multiplication tables. It wasn't the concept of multiplying that I had trouble with; it was memorizing the tables and then having to retrieve them quickly. I was not actually doing math, I was doing "rapid naming," which is a process that can create tremendous hurdles for dyslexic readers throughout their lives.

My father was in a car accident around this time, and he was laid up for a while. He committed himself to teaching me the times tables during his month-long convalescence. I could see the frustration in his eyes when I didn't know what I had known the day before.

We dyslexics all have good days and bad days, during which we learn more or less. Researchers don't yet know why.

I can't imagine what I would have done if he hadn't had the time to drill me. I improved, but to this day my multiplication tables are nothing to brag about. I still have to compute the answer rather than recall it. Oddly, and without any more difficulty than other doctoral candidates, I completed all the statistics programs required for my degree. Statistics requires conceptual thinking, and that's something I can do.

. . .

Dyslexia is strange. What may be simple for others is difficult for us, while what is difficult for others may be easy for us. Albert Einstein failed language-oriented subjects in school, yet he changed the world by developing his theories of special and general relativity. Difficult books may be easier for us to read than simple ones, because their intricate content keeps us interested. Simple books may bore us, because of how slowly we read.

Thankfully, the words we need to read and the multiplication tables we need to memorize are finite, not infinite. I was capable of progress. If I hammered away at it long enough, I would definitely make gains. It would be slow, painful progress, but progress nonetheless.

Never let people put you in a box.
Don't let what you can't do now predict your future.

Despite his being prone to anger after his accident, my father worked closely and patiently with me. He slowly came to understand that I wasn't learning to read. He knew I was struggling hard and was barely able to keep up with my class.

My father also saw me struggle at home. He worked in the insurance business, and he would bring home some of his work. He asked my sister and me to put his cards in alphabetical order. Before I filed each and every card, I had to repeat the alphabet in my head. He'd say, "What's the matter? Don't you even know the alphabet?" I was in third grade.

He knew something was wrong, and he figured it had something to do with the school and the teachers. He thought it must be *their* fault.

My father took time off from work to join my mother at parent-teacher night at my school. Mrs. Rhodes described the activities we were engaged in during the day. When she got to talking about the xylophone we were learning to play, my father lost his temper.

"A xylophone? A xylophone? What in the hell are you bothering her with a damned xylophone for? She needs to learn to read, not to learn some ridiculous instrument you hit with a mallet."

I was fast asleep when my parents returned home. My father tiptoed into my room and nudged me. I stirred. "Linnie," he half-whispered. "Mom and I just got back from school. I want you to know something. I straightened out that Mrs. Rhodes for you. Everything's going to be okay. Good night now."

Destroying the Enemy

One afternoon in fourth grade, I was handed a worksheet to complete. Everyone around me grabbed the paper and went to work. I couldn't even read the instructions, let alone do the work. It frustrated me to the extreme that day. The print was so small and there were so many words.

Didn't *anyone* know what it was like for me? *This really is impossible!* I was so angry that I grabbed a pencil, held it in my fist, and violently scribbled back and forth on the page with such force that the pencil point snagged the paper and tore it. It became a mangled piece of trash. I smoothed it out before I turned it in.

The next day, I was nervous about going to school but surprised that the teacher didn't say a word. I wondered why. And then it dawned on me. She hadn't been surprised, of course. She knew. The whole faculty knew. *Linda Greenbaum has a problem.*

Another day I cheated on a test. I could see my classmate Jane's paper so easily; I couldn't help it. I wanted to do well for a change. Jane was very smart, part of that clique of really smart students you have in every grade. On my way home from school, I felt relieved — not guilty as I might have expected. And I now know why. For once, I had answers. Good answers. Correct answers. The same answers a really bright student would have. And I didn't feel bad. I felt great.

That was on a Friday. On Monday, when I walked into school, I wasn't expecting any trouble from having cheated. I was plenty scared when, without saying a word, my teacher beckoned me out into the hall and into an empty classroom next door. She handed me the test again and said nothing other than, "Let me know when you're finished."

I was back to where I had started.

The Relief a Sick Day Brings

Individuals with learning disabilities are subject to a lot of sicknesses, especially asthma and allergies, which makes them more susceptible to – and slower to recover from – a cold or the flu. That's how it was for me, too.

Researchers aren't sure why. One theory is that the genes for asthma and allergies are somehow related to the genes for dyslexia. It's likely to turn out to be a combination of genetics, stress and environment, but then again, what isn't?

By the way, every successful dyslexic reader I've worked with also reports being sickly as a child. When we get out of school, we get instant relief from the stress of constantly playing catch-up, not getting what everyone else is getting, and being ashamed or embarrassed.

Mom-Mom Julie, who was so passionate about the people she loved, never let reality get in the way of seeing them in a positive light. She used to say the reason I was behind academically was because I was always out of school sick.

Sunday School? No Thanks

I cried hysterically every Sunday about going to religious school. This was new behavior for me. I had always been a good girl and a fairly compliant child.

I thank my parents for allowing me to drop out. All my cousins were going to religious school, and my parents really wanted me to go, but they were smart: They valued my experience and quality of life more than their need for me to conform. They saw how desperately upset I was, and they put my feelings before the social embarrassment of not having their daughter be where she was supposed to be.

Today, most religious organizations have programs in place
to help learning-disabled children deal with
the reading material used in their studies.

I missed not knowing much about my religion's history and culture. Years later, when I discovered books on tape, I made up for that.

Just Five – and That's It!

Back then, I had a weird habit that I didn't understand at the time.

We lived about two blocks from the public library. I went there all the time, usually by myself. It was a treat. I'd roam the stacks and say hello to the librarians and the children I knew from school. I really seemed to fit in. Hey, if you are wandering around in a library, how can you have any kind of reading problem?

I was acting the part. I felt like a trespasser who was not supposed to be there, but I loved it all the same. I would take a long, long time choosing my books. I took them off the shelves, looked at the covers, smelled them, and opened them to listen to the way the plastic protective covers cracked. Sometimes I couldn't even read the title. But books transported me into a fantasy world anyway. I didn't care if I could read or not! I loved books and libraries and the whole ambiance – the allure of thinking, learning and reading.

During his elementary school years, Richard Wyatt,
who had dyslexia, lived across the street from a science museum.
His family recalls that he was there so much it seemed like
he lived at the museum and only came home for meals.
He went on to become a world-famous scientist!

Here's something funny: There was a limit to how many books I could check out on each visit to the library. I once asked the librarian if I could take a few more. She didn't smile back. "Just five! And that's it!" she said, pointing a yellow pencil at the little sign that stated the limit – a sign I could not read. That was embarrassing, but the real problem was that I was frustrated by that limit, even though I couldn't read the books.

I had a ritual. When I'd get the books home, I'd put them on my desk, and there they would sit, untouched, until it was time to take them back. Maybe I couldn't read them, but books stimulated my imagination. And isn't that what reading is supposed to do? I couldn't read, but I knew how to keep my dreams alive.

HOW I BECAME A TERRIBLE SNOB

How I Became a Terrible Snob:
Junior High

In elementary school, things had been going pretty well – mostly because the environment permitted me to hide my learning disability. There was enough wiggle room, and I was getting better and better at wiggling. There were some things I couldn't do, but not enough to blow my cover or force me out into the open. Kids really didn't pay that much attention to each other's academic lives.

Socially, I was fine. I was the cute little chick with a contagious laugh that everybody liked. I was popular.

On the morning of my first day at Leeds Junior High, I woke up totally excited, thrilled at the adventure before me. There'd be new boys, and there was the excitement of becoming a teenager. It was going to be great.

The Facts of Life

I had very recently learned the facts of life. My mom, doing her motherly duty, had bought a book about sex, and we sat down together so she could read it to me. She was obviously uncomfortable with the subject. We were about a page away from the description of intercourse when she suddenly handed the book to me and said, "Linda, read the rest yourself!"

But I couldn't read the words.

I called my girlfriend and told her about "the book." We hopped on our bikes and agreed to meet in a garage, so nobody would see us with the book. She could read, and she read it to me. Thankfully.

My girlfriends and I had slept in rollers the night before our first day of school – after all, it was the 1950s. We had chatted about what we'd wear and agreed to meet at my house early.

The morning dawned warm and sunny. We walked together, laughing and giggling and greeting the other students we recognized.

When we arrived at school, we were all ushered into a huge auditorium. It was a thousand times bigger and noisier than the one at elementary school. We were guided to a row of seats.

Masking Academic Problems

People with dyslexia often learn to make social accommodations to mask their academic problems. This is how Mike Gravel disguised his dyslexia: "I finessed my way. I compensated with street smarts. I developed all the necessary polish to be a good politician." He went on to serve as the U.S. Senator from Alaska for two terms.

An administrator announced that he was going to call us up to the front in order of the section to which we were assigned. It didn't take me long to notice that every single one of my girlfriends was being called before me. A few minutes later I had a realization that hit me right between the eyes and way deep in my stomach: The sections were organized according to academic ability – and the smartest students were being called first.

Practically everyone in the room had been summoned. But not me. There were only a few stragglers left. I looked around. It looked like Skid Row: Thugs and punks with longish dirty hair, smirking, throwing things and laughing, not even knowing we were being called to a section. There were very few girls remaining, and none was a petite, frightened girl like me.

I felt like I was suffocating. I didn't want my friends to see me. I slunk as far down into my chair as I could, almost crumbling onto the floor. I felt like cold leftovers.

A few minutes later, the kids in my section marched through the hall – past the custodian's closet, the boiler rooms and some smelly bathrooms – to a dark and dingy classroom, the only self-contained section housed in the basement. I felt like I was being marched to my cell in a prison. It must have felt like a life sentence, because I distinctly recall thinking that my life was over.

I hadn't yet learned that we worry about what others think of us, when in fact others worry much more about themselves. We are all the stars of our own soap operas.

What made it more horrible was knowing that I was here because of my academic problem. That's why they put me here. The elementary school administrators had conferred with their junior high counterparts. The counselors were concerned that I was crawling into a shell of self-consciousness; to build confidence, it would be best if I were in the lowest academic setting, where I wouldn't be at the bottom of the heap. It was a nice thought, but how meaningful would my successes be if I were competing with kids who couldn't care less about learning? Their logic seems bizarre now, but maybe it made sense 45 years ago.

During the first few weeks of school, my girlfriends got together and formed a social club. I hung out with them, but it was awful. They would talk about their classes and their new friends and their cool teachers. I had to keep my mouth shut. They invited me to the next get-together, but I made an excuse.

They kept inviting me, but I would never show up. Ever. I was totally embarrassed. I didn't want to be around people, especially those who knew me. I didn't want to tell them who was in my class, and I thought they would ask.

I was with this same group of kids all day long – for every single class. Socially, I was atrophying. I couldn't talk to anyone. And I now know why: Part of me knew I belonged in that class.

I was hiding, and I was fearful that I would be found out. Now I really was in my shell, and every day that shell grew more structurally sound and more comforting. Breaking out would be a huge job.

A Lost Opportunity

Marc Zimmerman had been my boyfriend from first to sixth grade, but in junior high, I flat out ignored him. I was so mortified about my situation that I never spoke to him again. Of all the kids my age, I was closest to him, and yet I was still willing to hide from him.

When I met Marc later as an adult, he said he remembered me being his elementary school soul mate. He hadn't grown very tall by junior high, and he thought I avoided him because I had moved on to older boys. Nothing could have been further from the truth. I avoided him out of embarrassment. I really wanted to talk to him and be his friend, but I couldn't take the risk. There are times when all of us feel like we just don't fit in.

Then, a very strange thing happened. My old friends began to see *me* as a snob because I was avoiding them. They read my self-consciousness as superiority. That wasn't it, of course, but that was how it seemed to them.

In the course of a few short weeks, I had transformed myself from Miss Popularity to the Snob of Leeds Junior High.

A Lonely Place to Hide

It was 1961 and there I was – still at Leeds Junior High. I had made it through seventh and half of eighth grade, and kids were starting to think about high school. My options were Philadelphia High School for Girls (Girls' High), for which I couldn't possibly qualify, or Germantown High, which was too rough. Great.

Bizarre, confusing things were happening at Leeds, things I never expected. The kids in my section began to take to me. One day, while I was walking home from school, one of the hoods from another section began to harass me. Diddy, a gang leader who was in my classes, grabbed the guy by his shirt and warned him, "Never mess with her. As a matter of fact, whenever you see her, you cross the street and keep walking. Got it?" Years later, I was saddened to hear that Diddy died from an injury he received in a gang fight.

My science teacher would look stunned by the questions I asked in class – questions that showed I was thinking and figuring things out. I knew my science better than any of my classmates, and the teacher knew that. She was puzzled; she told me she couldn't understand why I was in this section.

I was in the lowest academic class, yet when the entire grade took a standardized map-reading test, I got one of the highest scores. Now the teachers were getting confused.

They knew I had a problem, but they didn't understand dyslexia. I did well on the map test because my understanding came from "reading" the map rather than reading the words. The brief sentences were easier for me. North, south, east and west were marked on the map with little arrows. With my ring, I was able to remember right from left. During the test, to keep myself oriented, I would turn the page according to the directions given in each question. I was surprised to see my classmates not turning their pages. I also did well because, for once, the test was not timed. I needed plenty of time to do my work, and I had it.

Days later, after the tests were graded, the teacher called me to her desk and accused me of cheating. The next day it must have dawned on the teacher. If Linda had the highest score, from whom could she have cheated? Even though she later apologized for the accusation, all I felt was the shame. I was angry about the box that everyone was always trying to jam me into – and how they'd get mad and make accusations when I didn't fit.

I never told anyone at home about my great score. They might not have understood either, because I surely didn't understand.

There was more: My petite physical stature contributed to my feeling overwhelmed – first academically, then socially and emotionally and, finally, physically.

One evening at dinner, I told my family the story about how Diddy had protected me. A dark expression crossed my mother's face. She suddenly pushed her chair back, stood up and looked at my father. She made a startling pronouncement. "Linda will not be subjected to that any longer! We're moving!" she said. We all fell silent.

"You will not go to Germantown High, where they'll stick you in another class like you're in now," my mom said. "Even the tutoring never helped. I'll do whatever I have to do to get you out of there. We'll move to Cheltenham Township. We'll move out of our house and live in an apartment if we have to." Cheltenham was known to have a great school system.

Money never flowed easily in our house. Most of my parents' arguments were over our finances. My father, who had learned lessons from the Depression, worked very hard and saved everything he could. He surprised us when he said we could afford to buy a nice single home in Elkins Park in Cheltenham Township right away. We didn't know he had accrued that much money.

That September I found myself attending the first day of ninth grade at Elkins Park Junior High. I was ecstatic to find out that instead of self-contained sections, my new junior high had a homeroom, and we all had individual rosters. No longer would my learning disability have to saturate my entire life and being. It was possible that I could be just who I was – beyond the walls of the remedial classroom in the basement.

Learning to socialize is critical. Part of my ability to be social
was a conscious decision after junior high. I knew that I had
to develop social skills so I could avoid being isolated.
I remember observing popular kids to see what they did,
hear what they said, and act the way they acted.

If You Think English Is Tough

In Spanish class, I received a gift – a "D" on my report card. My teacher was generous. No matter how hard I tried, I couldn't grasp Spanish. I was having enough trouble with English, and adding a foreign language into the mix … well, that was just too much.

I didn't earn that "D," or even close to it. But I did earn my teacher's respect. She knew I was working hard, and even though I couldn't master the material, my effort saved me. She simply didn't have the heart to flunk me. She probably had seen other students like me – ones that just didn't get it.

I got through school by sacrificing a lot of my time to work incredibly hard. I also benefited from the generosity of teachers. I had hit the lottery with that "D," and I knew it.

When Arthur Ochs Sulzberger, former publisher of
The New York Times*, first took up the study of Latin in school,*
the class participated in an annual Latin play. The best roles
were assigned to the most adept students and the minor roles
to the average students. Sulzberger played a mute slave.

Finding a Confidant

I was good at keeping secrets, and I had a big one: I was stupid. I wouldn't share that with anyone; I thought that telling someone would make it true for sure.

When I was 13, I went to overnight camp for one month. Camp Olympia, in Bucks County, PA, was a sports-oriented camp. I wasn't athletic – I was a slow runner with poor eye-hand coordination – and I couldn't find a place for myself. I hated it. I cried and cried, and I never went back.

During the summers, when most of my friends went back to camp, I stayed home, and I was lonely. For the first time ever, I shared my secret with two people. One was my best friend, Phyllis Green, who I nicknamed "P. Green." I didn't specifically tell her what my problem was. I simply wrote her a letter, and my poor writing and spelling gave me away. It wasn't a secret any longer. I knew that she wouldn't laugh at me. And if she did tease, it would be in a loving way.

I also wrote a letter to Denny Tessler, who I had met at Camp Olympia. I liked him right away. Denny was everything I wasn't: big, strong, articulate, confident and a star athlete at camp. That summer, he had told his friends that he "wasn't gonna mess around" with a young girl of 13 when he was a cool guy of 15. When we met again two years later at a Sweet 16, he asked me for a date. He had been my boyfriend ever since. Denny never commented on my pathetic letters.

. . .

I didn't know it at the time, but I'd later meet Arthur Ochs Sulzberger, the publisher of *The New York Times*. He had his confidant, too.

I traveled to New York to interview Arthur about how famous people cope with their dyslexia. To get in to see him, I had to walk past armed guards and go up a series of elevators. There were more guards on the top floor. Then, I walked down a very long hallway. On my left-hand side was a field of desks filled with secretary after secretary after secretary. This was part of the staging to see The Big Man. It was intimidating.

His receptionist asked me to wait, and finally I was ushered into his office. I found myself sitting across an immense desk from the sweetest, dearest man. He was so unassuming and warm.

Arthur told me how he gets around his dyslexia. It was amazing. "You see all of those secretaries out there?" he whispered. "None of them know. But do you see that one over there?" he said, pointing to one of them. "She's my confidante. Nothing goes out of this office without her checking it thoroughly."

Arthur went on to tell me that we dyslexic readers have certain innate talents, and that we are great at juggling big puzzles. These skills form the foundation of the conceptualizing and decision-making he does all the time. It's interesting to note that many engineers, who also depend on these skills, have dyslexia.

Arthur talked about his childhood. He was a nightmare for the family. He kept flunking out, but because his family was wealthy, they were able to move him from school to school. His father thought he was an idiot. His mother, who was very sympathetic, kept covering for him. She remembered that her own father had had similar problems. She recalled how her mother had covered for her father, with reading and writing and other things he wasn't good at doing.

As he was finishing, he told me that he thought his grandfather was probably a dyslexic reader, too. No one knew it then. No one had even heard of dyslexia. But that didn't stop the man from founding what may be the greatest newspaper in the world – *The New York Times*.

Spelling Problems

With remediation, many people with dyslexia can improve their reading skills and learn to enjoy reading, but spelling doesn't seem to respond as readily. It's often the last thing to be remediated, and many of us never become decent spellers.

Some of us don't care. Author Mark Twain didn't think very highly of "good spelling." Among his famous quotations is this one: "I never trusted people who couldn't think of more than one way to spell a word."

CHAPTER
13

SIX HUNDRED
AND SIXTY-THREE

Six Hundred and Sixty-Three:
High School

If it wasn't too hard to hide out at Elkins Park Junior High, you should have seen how easy it was to do so at Cheltenham High School.

Hiding was a recurrent theme in my life. I would keep my mouth shut and my head down. Then, I would do something and be found out. I'd go back into hiding until I was exposed again. It was a real struggle, and I was always worried that I'd get caught.

Tenth grade, my first year of high school, was great – a new school, more classes, more activities, and so many other teenagers. I consciously built a network of friends who went to nearby schools, because I was afraid the students at my school would find out that I was dumb. I dated boys from other schools for the same reason.

In eleventh grade, it was time to see the college guidance counselor. "You are not college material," he declared. Didn't he know that college was my goal? Didn't he know that I did homework for three to four hours every single day, whereas other kids might put in only 45 minutes? I guess not.

He told me that I ought to go to X-ray technician school. His idea floored me. I, who had dreams of college, couldn't believe my ears.

X-ray tech school was for students who weren't prepared to go to college. No one I knew was going there. I wanted to do what my friends were doing. I wanted to go where they were going. I didn't want to be isolated. I didn't want to be in a basement classroom again.

Then a plan flashed through my mind. I'd work harder than ever, so I could get a decent score on my SATs. And that's what I did. I worked so hard my mother was worried. She kept telling me to take a break, get some fresh air, or go to the movies or the Cheltenham Shopping Center with my friends. No way! I was focused on prepping for the SAT. There would be time for hanging out later.

I took the test. It was a nightmare. I could barely read it.

It was a four weeks before the score arrived in the mail. My mother didn't open the letter; she set it out on the dining room table. When I got home, she steered me to it. I was really nervous.

I opened the envelope. I knew the highest possible score – the perfect score – was 1600, 800 in the Verbal section and 800 in Math. I knew I didn't do so well, but when I saw a score that totaled 663, I had to blink a couple of times. I flipped the slip of paper over, hoping to see the rest of the score, maybe on the back. It was blank. That was it: 323 Verbal, 340 Math.

Generally, you need to break 1,000 for admission to college, but 663 was my combined score. Six hundred and sixty-three? Everyone knows you get an automatic 400 points just for showing up. Six hundred and sixty-three?

Into and Out of the Shadows

After it sank in that I was truly incompetent academically, I remembered the suggestion about X-ray tech school. I certainly didn't spell well enough to be a secretary. I couldn't do very many things, but they thought I could be an X-ray technician. Sure, it was honorable and important work, but it just wasn't for me. I couldn't do that kind of work. I had no faculty for mechanical things, and no interest, either. I was not physically strong, and the job required moving patients around on exam tables.

Even worse, I had my mother in my ear, anxious that I'd become dependent on some man. She couldn't stand that. She saw what had happened to women who were at the mercy of their husbands. She was always at me about finding a career and beginning to study for it. This was one of *her* unfulfilled dreams.

After graduating from high school in 1966, I found myself in the X-ray tech program at Hahnemann Hospital in Philadelphia. It was housed in dark and dank basement classrooms. Once again, my learning disability had landed me in a dreary place.

I had suspected that it wasn't for me, but once I was there, I *knew* it wasn't for me. It was horrible. To make things worse, the instructor turned out to be a nasty woman. One day she glared at me and announced to one and all, "Some of us may not be cut out for an X-ray technician career." I thought that was incredibly rude, insensitive and flat out hostile.

After one month, our progress in the program was evaluated. My report card arrived by mail on a Saturday, when I was at Penn State University visiting Denny. Although we went to different high schools and colleges, and although we dated other people, we always came back to each other. We made a point of seeing each other once a month.

I was plenty worried. I called home to ask if the review had come. "Sure, it's here," my parents said. "Everything seems fine. You can read the details when you get home." They rushed me off the phone. In fact, they had read the letter and didn't want to ruin my weekend.

When I got home Sunday night, I struggled to read the letter. It was nothing short of a disaster. After just one month, I was dismissed from the program for "academic reasons." I was angry at my parents for lying to me, and I was embarrassed to tell anyone, especially Denny. But when I did, he didn't care at all. "The hell with them," he said, "You don't need them." He told me he'd come home the very next weekend and we'd do something great. It made me feel a little better that it didn't bother Denny.

When I awoke the next morning, the upset from the day before came down on me. I got out of bed anyway. I carried my pain with me and marched myself over to the Lord & Taylor department store in Jenkintown. I applied for a job, and I was hired immediately.

I was unconsciously already using the Six Clues to Successfully Managing a Learning Disability – this one being the principle of staying in action. Keep moving! The world rewards activity.

The very next day, I began working as a salesgirl. Management took notice that I was capable and that I could do more. When the professionals were busy, they had me decorating windows and organizing fashion shows.

I was using my creativity and my brain. For the first time, I was able to see that I had an ability that produced something of value – and I was far away from the written word.

Before then, all I saw were mistakes and flubs and struggles just to break even. Doing windows and fashion shows in a gorgeous, open and airy department store – and getting praised and paid for it – was a new experience. It sure beat being tormented by a mean-spirited X-ray class instructor; wearing a heavy, smelly lead apron; and trying to read the dials on battered old hospital equipment.

And what about that 663? Last time I checked, I had gotten through college and graduate school, earned a master's degree and a doctorate, and established a successful practice. Six hundred and sixty-three? It's only number on a piece of paper that's been buried under tons of trash in a garbage dump in the middle of nowhere for the last 40 years!

Six hundred and sixty-three? What's that got to do with me?

CHAPTER 14

THE FIGHT

I now know that my outburst was not directed only at my mother, but also at all my teachers, my friends and my family. It was about not being able to read the books I got from the library, at being put in that horrible classroom in the basement. It was about the tech school instructor and her snide comment, "Not all of our students are X-ray tech school material."

The Fight

When I was 17, I had an ugly and passionate encounter with my mother. Neither one of us knew what was going on or why. Years later, I came to understand that this is the kind of fight dyslexic readers almost always have if they are fortunate enough to have someone in their lives who believes in them.

Just a few weeks had passed since I got kicked out of X-ray technician school. Actually, I flunked out. Getting kicked out sounds better. It sounds like I misbehaved, but the truth was, I couldn't cut it there.

I was working at the department store, and I was doing fine. I was able to exercise my creative side and make some money. But when I was unoccupied, the dark thoughts came. I was despondent.

The Battle Royal began when my mother and I were doing dishes. I was washing; she was drying and putting the dishes away in the cabinets.

"What's the matter?" she asked. She had noticed that I was unusually quiet. I must have seemed distracted, too.

"X-ray tech school, Mom," I said. "That's not a course where you have to be a genius to pass, and I flunked out. I'm worried about my future, I guess. It's embarrassing to flunk out of there."

My mom put her wet dish down on the counter and turned to me. I didn't look up. "Linda, I don't want to hear you talk like that, and I certainly don't want you thinking like that."

"Well, that's how I feel. That's the truth."

"That's crazy," she said, throwing a soggy dishrag into the sink. "You have to remember one thing, Linda. You *are* smart! You are clever and very creative. You have a wonderful imagination. Don't let a few problems in school or trouble reading make you think otherwise."

I turned off the water that had been running in the sink. My face turned red, and white-hot anger rose up in me.

"What makes you say that?" I was practically screaming. Tears were already blurring my vision. "What the hell makes you say I am smart? The only proof there is, is that I am stupid! *Stupid!*"

My mother's mouth dropped open. A rare moment of speechlessness. She had never heard me talk like this, and I had never heard myself speak to my mother this way. I was enraged at my mother in a way that I had never been enraged before.

"What on earth allows you to come to the conclusion that I am smart?" I asked.

What was she talking about? There was so much evidence to the contrary. She stood there, stunned. That didn't stop me in my rage. Her silence was my clue to keep going.

"Why don't you stop having this fantasy of who I am? I'm not good enough to do anything. I'm not your little fantasy of the perfect brilliant daughter majoring in premed. I'm stupid little Linda Greenbaum, too dumb to even make it out of tech school."

"Linda," my mom began, but I told her to shut up with the wave of my hand.

"No!" I screamed, crying. "No! *You* listen to *me!*"

I couldn't be stopped. "You're not seeing who I am. You live in a fantasy world. You always say I am smart. I hear you on the phone talking to your friends, saying, 'Linda's doing fine. I'm so proud of the way she picked herself up and got a job. She's such a bright kid.' But I wonder, Linda *who*?"

"You calm down!" she said, pointing a finger.

"I don't want to hear you say that again, Mother. Do you hear me? I never, ever, ever, ever, ever want to hear that from you again. I'm not who you want me to be. Got it? I'm nowhere. I can't do *anything* you think I can do."

On a winter's night, you may be warm and toasty under the covers,
but it's not far from your mind that it's freezing outside,
and that if you had to venture out, it would be cold and dark.

I had done something I didn't know I could do. I had screamed at my mother with venom. I still feel bad about it, because I know my mother would never intentionally do anything to hurt me.

I ran from the room. I think I knocked over a kitchen chair on my way out. I bounded up the stairs, flew into my room, kicked the door shut and fell onto my bed sobbing. I didn't understand what had happened.

About 10 minutes later, I heard one loud bang on my door. It was made by an angry fist. Then, my mother's voice.

"Don't talk to me like that," she said through the door. Her voice was very controlled – and that scared me. I could hear the tears hiding under her voice. She was furious and deeply hurt and confused.

"And don't raise your voice to me, either," she said. There was a long pause. "And one more thing. You *are* smart. I know what I'm talking about."

Then there was silence. I heard her footsteps as she walked away.

I wanted to explain more to her, about how I felt and who I was, but I didn't have the words. My disappointments and frustrations were stuck in my throat. Sometimes there are no words for the deepest emotions.

I stayed in my room all night. The next thing I knew, it was morning. I awoke with a terrible thirst. I had slept in my clothes. After I took a shower, I went downstairs, anxious about seeing my mother. I could hear her working in the kitchen.

I had been honest and had spoken from my gut, but that didn't make me feel any better.

I sat down at the breakfast table. I was ashamed to look up. I just sat there for a minute moving my fork and napkin around, and then my mother spoke.

"Linda," she said in the voice I had known all my life. "Orange juice or milk?"

...

Years ago, I saw a movie about a boy with a learning disability. He had the same exact fight with his family. When someone believes in you, and you don't believe in yourself, this kind of conflict is inevitable. Their inflated image of you makes you angry. You feel bad that you can't meet their high expectations.

But the truth is, we all need someone to have faith in us. My mom had an indomitable belief in me. She had studied me in order to observe my strengths, not my weaknesses. Then she mirrored my strengths back to me – not smothering me, not doing for me, not solving problems for me, but just believing in my ability to handle my own life. That made a big difference in my growth as a human being.

CHAPTER 15

DEFINING MOMENTS

Defining Moments

There are moments in each of our lives when we can choose between two paths. Although the decision we make may be conscious or unconscious, our choice can set the course for our life.

On one path, you take responsibility for yourself and what happened to you. You examine your strengths. You build a life based on those strengths and do damage control for your weaknesses. You stay in action. You take your fear and sadness with you, but they don't control you.

If you go in the other direction, you blame others, you blame the circumstances, and you focus on your inabilities. You end up feeling hopeless, which is the ultimate definition of hell – having no hope. On this road, you pay a toll: You convince yourself that you don't have choices. You feel powerless. You feel sorry for yourself. You give your power and spirit away to circumstance.

At a critical moment, it's simply easier to take the path of blaming others and blaming circumstances. It feels safe, but in truth, it is much riskier. On the other road, the tougher road, there is plenty to worry about: It is an unfamiliar path to the unknown.

Sometimes, failure serves as a message: It lets us know that we might need to do something different. My failure in X-ray technician school brought me to a decision point, a fork in the road.

Teach yourself to recognize when these critical moments appear. Then dig down deep to find and *use* your courage. If you can't find any, look again. It's in there somewhere. Focus. Trust.

For me, the focus was on going to college. I had put aside that goal, but I still yearned for it. Graduating was a different matter – and far down the road. I stayed focused on the present because that's where I found my strength.

I needed to be where *I* wanted to be, not where others thought I should be. I had looked the possibility of not finishing school squarely in the face. If I didn't make it, I would at least fail while trying to do what I wanted to do. I had never wanted to be an X-ray technician.

I would go to college. It scared me deeply, but it didn't stop me.

CHAPTER **16**

DO NOT ENTER ZONES

Do Not Enter Zones:

Avoiding Depression and Anxiety

It's stressful to live with a learning disability, and those of us who do so are prone to anxiety and depression. We all experience these feelings from time to time – because we are *thinking* all of the time. It is the content of these thoughts that can produce anxiety and depression or, for that matter, happiness and joy. Sadness is also part of the picture, as people suffering with anxiety may feel sad that they don't have a sense of well-being.

Please note that this sadness is not to be confused with clinical depression, which needs to be treated by a professional.

Do Not Enter Zones

Anxiety and depression can be greatly reduced if the behaviors that cause them are eliminated or controlled. I call these behaviors "Do Not Enter Zones" or "Thought Potholes."

Remember that you are responsible for your thoughts. You're the one who frightens yourself, and you must be the one who calms yourself. The happy truth is that most situations are not nearly as desperate or threatening as the anxious or depressed person perceives.

Although at times your learning disability might leave you feeling stupid or like a loser, you are neither: You are a normal person with human weaknesses and with very real abilities and talents.

PERFECTIONISM

Human beings aren't perfect. Making everything perfect is an impossible goal and a ticket to depression. The value in what you do far outweighs the imperfections. Hand in that term paper. Let it go. Go on that job interview. Who cares if you don't get the job? Learn whatever you need to learn from the experience.

 ## LACK OF ASSERTIVENESS

When you feel that you have no control over a situation, you feel anxious. When you speak and act assertively, a sense of control returns and anxiety or depression decreases.

There are important differences between assertiveness, aggressiveness, and passiveness. Assertiveness, or self-care, should not be confused with selfishness. When you take care of yourself first, you conserve your strength to help others – just as in an airline emergency, an adult should don an oxygen mask first so he will be able to help a child. In contrast, aggressiveness is when you take care of yourself at the expense of others.

Passivity is when you allow things to happen at *your* expense. Bear in mind that you have needs, too, and that you are responsible for getting them met. Assertively advocate for yourself with your spouse, your boss and your teachers. Tell them what you need without apologizing for yourself.

Children also need to feel a sense of control and be allowed to make age-appropriate decisions. Assertive parents and teachers provide a model for children, inspiring them to take charge of their own lives.

UNREALISTIC EXPECTATIONS

Set reachable goals for yourself. Then create realistic expectations as to how much you can accomplish in a day. Learning even one new word should be regarded as a small success. What's important is that you learn, not that you learn quickly. While one person may learn something with just one repetition, another may need a hundred repetitions. So what?

Those who need more time to learn a task can master it as well as, or even better than, those who learn in less time. Reaching your goal is important; the fact that you took a few detours along the way is not.

You can get to the Promised Land in a Volkswagen or a Mercedes. It doesn't matter, as long as you get there.

On the other hand, don't sell yourself short. Set your goals as high as possible. I'm not talking about striving for perfection; I'm talking about being inspired by your own excellence.

Dr. Charles Drake, founder of the nation's first college for students with dyslexia, believes that expectations of people with learning disabilities are too low. He was referring to our expectations of LD students *and* their expectations of themselves. A learning disability should never be an excuse for bad behavior, inadequate performance, or for not utilizing your strengths.

When setting a goal, avoid tunnel vision. Consider what you truly want to gain. What thoughts, feelings or experiences will it provide for you? Should the goal prove unrealistic, another can be substituted, which will provide many of the same rewards.

A patient in my practice had set a goal of becoming a pharmacist, but in pharmacy school, she found that her learning disability made it very difficult to pass certain types of exams. As a result, she suffered from severe anxiety. On closer examination of her goal, she realized that she had picked pharmacy because she had a strong desire to do humanitarian work that was financially rewarding and enjoyable. Once she uncovered her motivation, she was able to identify several other fields that might be easier for her but that offered the same rewards.

Knowing that she had a "Plan B" greatly lowered her anxiety, which in turn increased her performance. She may yet become a successful pharmacist, but if not, she will still do fulfilling, financially rewarding work, even if it is in another field.

 WORRYING ABOUT THE FUTURE

Being overly concerned about problems that could occur in the distant future is paralyzing and useless. An example is a 12-year-old obsessively dwelling on the question, "What if I can't get into college?" Instead, think about how you can do your best now. Contemplate the future to the extent that it's useful. Bear in mind that 90 percent of the things we worry about never happen.

 BLAME

When you feel depressed and anxious, you may look outside yourself and blame other people, institutions, the workplace, school, or family. Or, you may blame yourself. You may say mean things to yourself that you would never say to a friend. If you find yourself in this rut, try being kind to yourself. You may even have to ask yourself for forgiveness.

It's as if you have a broken leg. You need to be responsible for it, perhaps by going to the doctor to get it set. It's not useful to blame yourself or others. The healing begins when you take responsibility.

 ## OBSESSIVE THINKING

When a particular problem is dominating your thoughts way beyond the time you set aside for problem solving, you're impeding your own progress. Sometimes we use obsessive thoughts to distract us from something that is truly bothering us on a less conscious level. If you get quiet enough, you will discover what is really bothering you.

 ## VICTIM THINKING

Feeling sorry for yourself is self-defeating. It will never get you anywhere. If you must have a "pity party," keep it brief, and then get on with living life. Don't waste time dwelling on what you can't do.

 ## OVERREACTING

Keep things in perspective. The problem you face today will usually resolve itself. Sometimes someone close to you will need to remind you to get out of this pothole. If you want to try to change perspective yourself, imagine you are on a plane high in the sky looking down on your life. Doesn't that give you a different view of your situation?

No matter what you do, 20 percent of the people will like you, 20 percent won't like you, and the other 60 percent will fall somewhere in between. That's not bad!

 ## OVERSENSITIVITY TO CRITICISM

No one likes to be criticized, but when you are, consider whether you can use the criticism to better yourself – and then move on. What you think of yourself is important. What others think of you is not nearly as critical. Just because someone says, "You are not trying" or "You're being careless" doesn't make it true.

What to Do When You Feel Anxious and Depressed

You will, at times, feel anxious or depressed. After you have done what you can to correct the situation, it is time to deal with your feelings. Try this process:

1. Recognize that something is bothering you and give yourself permission to feel the way you do. To deny the feeling is not helpful. Of course, most people would like to skip this part. Don't. If you skip Step 1, the process will not work.

2. Be your own best friend. Speak to yourself using truthful, compassionate statements.

3. Think about the worst thing that could happen as a result of this problem.

4. What does this situation remind you of from your past?

5. Now think about the best thing that could happen as a result of this problem. Make a mental picture; hear the sound and feel the feelings of the best thing that could happen.

6. Hold on to that picture. Keep it with you.

...

It's possible to create habits of healthy thinking that lead to healthy behavior and a dramatic decrease in anxiety and depression.

Remember the beautiful pearl I lost? I had dwelt on it for months. I had given up searching for it. I knew it was gone, but I wasn't able to get it out of my mind. I felt guilty, as though I had lost it intentionally. My guilt was keeping me stuck. It prevented me from letting go and moving on.

Then one day I consciously sat down and made peace with the idea that a generous gift had come and gone. I talked to myself. "After all," I said, "everything is only temporary." I decided that life was too short to spend any more time on "the lost."

...

You, too, can make peace with the things that get you down. Most issues are more difficult to let go of than my pearl was, but the process is the same. Find a positive thought to replace your negative thought. Uncovering that constructive thought is actually more taxing than letting go.

Learning to change one's thinking patterns is not easy work, but it is life-changing work. It requires practice, but the good news is that we get better at whatever we practice. Practice responding to yourself respectfully, kindly, comfortingly and compassionately.

If you are still in a rut or clinically depressed, make an appointment with a psychologist or a psychiatrist. There are also fine books and courses on the topic. Two that have greatly contributed to my own thinking are *Attacking Anxiety and Depression* from the Midwest Center for Stress and Anxiety and *The Anxiety and Phobia Workbook* by Edmund J. Bourne, Ph.D.

College Bound?

"When I talk to college students about all of this, I tell them to work with their strengths, not their weaknesses. If you're not good at reading, do something else. Go where you are strong."

- Paul J. Orfalea, a dyslexia reader who founded Kinko's copy shop in 1970 and transformed it into a $2 billion a year company.

CHAPTER 17

TOUR GUIDE, AT YOUR SERVICE

"Feel the fear –
and do it anyway."
– Anonymous

Tour Guide, at Your Service

I needed help. I needed an angel.

After the humiliation of flunking out of X-ray tech school and the realization that my job at Lord & Taylor was a dead end, it became as clear as glass that I needed to find someone to help me with my reading and writing – if I ever wanted to get ahead.

Sometimes the things you need are right under your nose. That was the case with Joseph Mathern, Ph.D., a wonderful, generous man who, with his wife, rented a modest apartment one floor below my grandparents. He was the retired head of the English department at a local university.

He was gentle and kind, and I felt safe telling him about my reading and writing troubles. He didn't hesitate to say that he'd be happy to help me.

"You just come here as many days a week as you want, and for as long as you can stand it, and I promise I will help you learn to read," he said.

He said something else, too. "You know what you need. You tell me and we'll figure it out together. Let me be your vehicle to get you where you want to go. I'll know you are improving before you do." Dr. Mathern gave me hope.

He wanted no money, but I couldn't let him give me so much without reciprocating. At one point during each tutoring session I would slide a $5 bill under the green blotter on his desk.

I must have seen him three or four times a week; our sessions sometimes lasted up to three hours. I'd work – and he'd work – until my brain was fried and my head literally hurt. No matter how long I was able to go on, so was he.

Dyslexic readers are prone to mental fatigue, probably because their brain needs to take longer pathways.

It was so hard for me to read. I would read so slowly that sometimes I would get just halfway down a page during the session. One day as I was leaving, Dr. Mathern held a book in his hand and said, "Linda, it's okay that it's taking you so long to read. Do you know how long it took the writer to write a good page?"

From that day on, when I sit down to read a book, I think: I'm just going to read this page and take my time. I read with that mental attitude.

I don't know how I could have gotten to where I am today without Dr. Mathern.

Maybe I couldn't have. But isn't that what angels are for?

CHAPTER **18**

GETTING BACK ON THE ROAD

Getting Back on the Road

I had been working at Lord & Taylor for a few months. Things had calmed down, but I still felt lost. I was living at home and making some money, but I was cut off socially. I had no direction.

That got rubbed in one day around the holidays when Marc Zimmerman's mother came into the store. I was well aware that Marc, my elementary school boyfriend, was in a premed program, while I was ringing up ladies' undergarments and dusting Christmas-themed display windows with fake snowflakes.

Everyone I knew was in college, and that's where I wanted to be. I had gained confidence in the three months I worked with Dr. Mathern, so I did something about it. In January 1967, I began taking night classes at St. Joseph's University in Philadelphia. I had no idea how I was going to get through college, but I was going to try.

Luckily, my psychology class used a relatively thin textbook. I chose to become obsessed with that book. I spent almost all of my spare time reading it, one word at a time, underlining, asking the professor a lot of questions, and paying close attention in class.

I never missed a class. I spent an inordinate amount of time reading, yet I never finished everything and never completely understood all the words I read.

My English composition class was a problem: I couldn't come up with 12 years of reading and writing skills overnight. On the day of the English exam, I was literally trembling. To calm myself down I closed my eyes and imagined I was looking into Denny's eyes – the way you look into the eyes of someone who you trust to accept you as you are. That helped.

Before the test, the teacher asked to see me in the hall. "Do they speak a foreign language at home?" he asked out of earshot of the other students.

"Yes," I lied.

He nodded and gave me an understanding smile. Then he took out a marker and wrote something on a piece of paper. "Okay, you can return to your seat," he said. A few days later, he passed out the graded exams. He had given me a C. That grade was a gift, pure and simple. I had English comp under my belt and an A in psychology, which I earned by working extremely hard and memorizing the book.

Now I could apply to college. I set my sights on Mills College of Education, a small school in Manhattan. It was a good fit for me. I could chalk up two years of student-teaching experience before I graduated. I'd get more personal attention than in a large university, and I wouldn't have to retake the SATs.

I had dreamed of being a teacher since fifth grade. Teachers could read. They were the smartest people in the world. I also was particularly inspired by my teacher, Mrs. Keif, who was so kind to me. She had known that something was wrong, so she had me tested. Although my reading score was horrible, the IQ test showed that I was very bright.

In elementary school, the best students would get the fun jobs. I hadn't ever been one of them until fifth grade, when Mrs. Keif would pick *me* to decorate the bulletin boards. Suddenly, I had strengths. She got me to feel good about myself. She was the first teacher to believe in me.

I was accepted to Mills, and in the fall of 1967, about 14 months after I graduated from high school, I began my classes. It was fantastic.

Through the years, being a teacher had seemed like the impossible dream, but here I was in college in New York City. (Dr. Mathern had worked with me all through my time at St. Joseph's University until I went off to Mills.)

I was completely engaged in my education and psychology classes. The conversations were stimulating, and I could speak out using my intellect, not burdened by having to read or write words. I learned how to prioritize my reading, because I knew I couldn't do it all. I learned to anticipate what would be on the test. I knew how to psych out the professors, and I made certain they knew I was committed to doing everything possible for the class. (This is something I recommend for every student with a learning disability.)

It was a big moment for me when I handed in my first college paper. I was scared to death. The writing and spelling were horrible, and I had a history of being humiliated when I submitted papers. But somehow, I let go of my fear just long enough to hand in the paper. I hoped to get feedback that although the writing was poor, my ideas had value.

That's exactly what happened.

Throughout college, teachers would often say to me, "There is such a huge difference between how you present yourself in class and how you present yourself on paper" – even though I already had my papers typed and my sentences untwisted by typists.

Still, I was getting As and Bs. I learned that there was more to me than just terrible writing and horrible spelling. In this academic environment, for the first time, I was making the grade.

CHAPTER 19

A SPEED-READING REJECT

A Speed-Reading Reject

After my satisfying, self-esteem-building experience with Dr. Mathern in Philadelphia, I did better than average in my freshman, sophomore and junior years at Mills. My confidence was being fortified daily. For the first time, I had come out of hiding without being flushed out.

During my junior year, I thought I'd supercharge my progress by signing up for the Evelyn Wood Speed-Reading Program. Before you enroll, they give you a test to see where you stand. The man who reviewed my test came out of his office and sat next to me at the table where I had taken the test minutes earlier.

"Sorry, Miss," he said, matter of factly. "We can't accept you. You don't read well enough to take this course." I was crushed. I walked out without saying another word.

How could that be? Hadn't I improved at all? How could I get As and Bs in college but not be smart enough to attend some reading class *that I had to pay for?*

The Evelyn Wood employee referred me to the NYU reading clinic, where I was tested again. The evaluator informed me that I was reading on a third-grade level.

"What?"

"Yes. The results are accurate," she insisted. "A third-grade reading level." The woman's bedside manner was horrible. She seemed completely devoid of any sensitivity whatsoever – or at least that's how it felt to me.

She said it was hard for her to believe that I really was in college and doing as well as I said. She casually predicted that I would never be able to graduate. She was clueless about how that news could devastate.

She bashed to a bloody pulp much of the confidence I had built up. I questioned my ability and past achievements. I never went back. I couldn't face it – or her – and didn't know what to do with my emotional reaction. I was overwhelmed, so I simply blocked it out.

Funny thing about failing to face your fears: They usually come back to haunt you. Had I gone back to the NYU reading clinic, who knows what I would have learned or what progress I would have made?

Back at Mills, despite my disability, I was carrying a solid 3.25 average. A big part of my success was that I was studying material for which I had an aptitude – teaching. It didn't hurt that I loved what I was doing and believed that I had something worthwhile to give.

I became even better at screening courses to avoid those with excessive amounts of reading: The less reading the better for me.

Mills allowed me to get out of the classroom and into the real world as a student teacher. I wanted a spot in a kindergarten, first- or second-grade class. I didn't want to tangle with fourth or fifth graders. They could read better than I could.

I found a great kindergarten classroom in a Manhattan public school. I was able to take my experiences and my struggles and incorporate them into my lesson plans. I instinctively used what I later learned was called *multisensory teaching*, which allowed my students to hear, see and actually do what they were learning.

The teacher who supervised me wrote a glowing report about what a wonderful teacher I would be. No one knew about my reading problem. I received a great evaluation, in part because I had struggled so much as a student that I was sensitive to what children really need from their teachers.

In May 1971, I graduated from Mills College of Education – in spite of what my high school guidance counselor had said and in spite of what the NYU reading clinic evaluator had predicted. Not college material? Hah!

Dancing for Joy

As a child, whenever I was upset, I would turn on music and dance in the basement. Dancing was my way of handling the stress I met head on every day of my life, but when I learned a routine in dance class, I would go in the wrong direction!

At Mills I decided to take a dance class in the Martha Graham modern dance technique. In modern dance, it mattered less whether I went left or right! Dancing provided more than a physical release. It was also an emotional and spiritual release. I was good at it. It was fun, and it had nothing to do with my language struggles. Today, I do ballroom dancing, and my partners keep me going in the right direction.

A Good
Balancing Act

*"Don't be afraid to dream big.
Concentrate on all that is possible
and go for it. Who knows where
those dreams will take you."*

- Debbie Macomber, dyslexic mother of four
and best-selling American author of over 150
romance novels and contemporary women's
fiction.

CHAPTER **20**

MARRIAGE, MOTHERHOOD, AND A MASTER'S DEGREE

Marriage, Motherhood and a Master's Degree

One week after I graduated from college, Denny and I were married. We had dated off and on for seven years. It had been a passionate and turbulent relationship, and my mother thought I was crazy to marry someone with whom I fought so much. But I knew better. No matter what, Denny was never judgmental about my academic troubles. When I flunked out of X-ray tech school, he didn't think I was stupid.

Statistically, people with learning differences tend to marry each other. We were no different. Even though Denny was very bright, he never applied himself in school. He couldn't concentrate or sit still in class, and he probably had Attention Deficit Disorder. But he was a talented athlete – a nationally ranked high jumper in high school – and that enabled him to get into Pennsylvania State University. At the beginning of the first semester, students were given a test that was supposed to predict their first-year cumulative average. The test indicated that Denny would fail out. It was wrong.

We're a great match in many ways, including that Denny is an excellent sight reader and he writes well, and I'm organized. He appreciates that I keep his world organized. As Rocky said to Adrian in *Rocky I*, "We fill in each other's gaps."

In September, I started my career as a second-grade teacher at Whitemarsh Elementary School in suburban Philadelphia. The newer teachers got the slower classes, which was perfect for me. I sympathized with the children who had trouble, and their reading improved significantly.

Among the students and parents, I was a popular teacher. I loved learning, and that was contagious.

I took my weaknesses – my lemons, so to speak – and made lemon-ade by turning them into games. For example, I asked my students to be "word detectives." Occasionally, I would make a spelling mistake on the board. Whoever spotted it first would get extra credit, which second graders loved.

By December, I was pregnant with my first child, Keith.

...

The Commonwealth of Pennsylvania required that teachers get graduate credits to maintain their licenses. To do so, I wanted to take classes at Villanova University. Happily, my high grade point average from undergraduate school enabled me to get into Villanova's master's degree program without having to sit for the Graduate Record Exam (GRE). Considering my struggles with the SAT, my GRE score would have probably been equally appalling.

I always did the best I could because I needed to bank those plusses to offset the big minus I carried around with me. Getting into Villanova was just another payoff for that work.

Once again, some crack in the universe opened up and helped me move forward.

To be successful, I needed to have a dependable support person to do damage control for my language weaknesses. Without someone to help me with my writing, I wouldn't make it at Villanova.

It took me over a year to find a person I could trust. (In those days, there was no Internet, which would have helped me locate someone much faster.) I had all kinds of mishaps, including a tutor whose bright idea was to hand me a grammar book and instruct me to read it carefully.

Finally, I found a retired English teacher, Knowles Cooke. He stuck with me through my master's and doctoral degree studies – a long 16 years of graduate work. He would read to me and correct my work, but he gave me something much more important: He believed in me.

It's All My Mother's Fault

I loved the entire process of earning my master's degree, but I didn't do it on my own, as I've written throughout these chapters. There is one culprit in particular behind all of this – and I say that affectionately.

I blame my mother. She instilled in me a real a love of learning. But if you love learning and have dyslexia, your ways of obtaining information are limited. Going for my master's degree was a way to keep learning and expand my horizons.

At Villanova, I worked on my master's degree one course at a time – at the same time that I was raising Keith, loving my husband, and maintaining my home. I had the benefit of challenging classroom sessions and one-on-one conversations with stimulating professors and bright, interesting adults.

I could never read everything that was assigned for the course, but I absorbed more than enough to master the material and the concepts. I was a straight-A student. For the first time, I could hold my own. I could *easily* hold my own. I was where I wanted – no, needed – to be.

I completed my master's work, graduating with a 4.0 grade point average and membership in the Phi Kappa Phi Honor Society.

I'm not bragging. I'm just illustrating why I had legitimate reasons to believe that I could succeed in attaining my doctorate. I had proven to myself that if I had extra time to get my work done, I would be free to expand my mind and get a valuable education.

Having Options

My parents were the children of immigrants, and they had lived through the Depression. My mother's constant refrain to me and my sister, Barbie, was that we absolutely had to learn to be financially independent and to care for ourselves. She wanted us to have options, so we'd never have to endure any relationship or situation that was toxic. Her words motivated me as well.

"You cannot afford to wait for perfect conditions. Goal setting is often a matter of balancing timing against available resources. Opportunities are easily lost while waiting for perfect conditions."

- Gary Ryan Blair, president of *The GoalsGuy Learning Systems*

DR. LINDA?

All my life, at every crossroad,
I've tried to choose the option
that would give me more self-respect,
even though that usually meant
a harder road to travel.

Dr. Linda?

On graduation day in the spring of 1977, I held my diploma: a Master's Degree in Guidance and Counseling from Villanova University. I also held my newborn second son, Brian.

My life had revolved around working, raising my children and going to school. How could they graduate me? I wanted to keep learning in this intense and challenging environment.

School was the right choice for me in so many ways. Denny was busy: He was devoted to building his business for the family. He had a passion to ride and he became a horseman. I was sometimes bored and lonely, but I wanted to be a stay-at-home mom, rather than get a job outside the home. (In the mid-1970s, the majority of mothers in my community stayed home to raise their children. My friends thought that graduate school was a "nice hobby." In fact, I was one of the few women in my doctoral classes.)

I knew more than ever that I would try for my doctorate, which required candidates to finish their course work within six years. I was slower at learning than others. I had better start strategizing or there would be no way I could make it. But if I didn't make it, I wouldn't care. I just wanted to be in school. I would enjoy the process no matter what happened.

I decided on Temple University, which had a great doctoral program in psychological studies and a flexible enough course of study that I could go part-time. Even better, when I researched the requirements, I discovered that I could take three non-matriculating courses – nine credits – before the clock started ticking on the six-year deadline. That would give me 18 extra months, which I would definitely need.

My first course was the Psychology of Group Processing, taught by Dr. Susan Wheelan, one of the most respected professors in the department. She took time to give me some very important feedback. After reading my paper, she wrote me a note saying that my work had given her some new insight.

What was that? My work gave her insight? *Was I reading that right?* Not long after, her doctoral assistant wrote something similar. Their feedback was critically important in my deciding to stay on course and continue to work toward my degree. It confirmed my hope that I was competent and might have something to contribute to this field.

One night a week Denny would watch the children and I would go to school. During the day, when Denny was at work and Brian and Keith were napping, I studied. It was intellectually demanding. By the time they woke up, it was time to rest my brain and get back to the kids. Perfect timing, but it was no accident. It was by design. I had constructed a wonderfully balanced life.

I finished the first two of my three non-matriculating doctoral courses, and I aced them both.

Here's a metaphor: As kids we love to build sand castles.
We take great pleasure and pride in shaping them.
But in an hour or two, the rising tide washes them away.
That's okay. Enjoy the process. Life is a process.

It was time to apply to Temple's doctoral program and to sit for the Graduate Record Exam. Even if I had been diagnosed with dyslexia by this time, I wouldn't have had any learning accommodations (such as having the test read to me), because no one had thought of it yet. Not surprisingly, my score was terrible. My 4.0 average from Villanova and in my doctoral courses, along with great recommendations, weren't enough to get me in. I was rejected because of the GRE score.

That rejection was a real flat tire. Still, I was proud of myself for a good effort, even though it failed. I knew I would have regretted it if I had been too afraid to apply. Even though I was rejected from the doctoral program, I had self-respect.

Finding Happiness

In family therapy theory, the mother is considered the emotional barometer of the family. If momma isn't happy, nobody's happy!

We are responsible for finding our own happiness, but where do we find it? Many people confuse happiness with comfort, but comfort doesn't make you happy. In fact, you get used to comfort, take it for granted, and then feel unhappy when you're not completely comfortable.

Happiness comes from something that is deeply and inherently satisfying, and it serves as an internal guidance system that helps us find purpose in life. For me, happiness is learning – and sharing what I learn with others. I've discovered that my joy comes when I am stimulated, focused and living in the moment.

A DIAGNOSIS AT LAST

Dyslexia

A Diagnosis at Last

I was taking a leisurely walk across campus, happy to be finishing up the last of my three non-matriculating courses. I had just watched Olympian Bruce Jenner talking about his dyslexia on TV on the *Phil Donahue Show*. Was this what I was experiencing? By chance, I looked up and saw that I was walking past Temple University's Office for the Disabled.

Could that be me? But the name – Office for the Disabled – didn't sit well with me. I had to get past the sign on that door. Was *I* disabled?

My fear of embarrassment made me hesitate, but I opened the door and walked inside anyway. If my only reason for not doing something is fear, then I do it.

Behind the desk was a man in a wheelchair and a woman who seemed to be the manager. She was well-informed, compassionate and knowledgeable about dyslexia. It was remarkable. She asked me questions that told me she was zeroing in on my problem.

She told me that if I had dyslexia, I could have the GRE read to me. I remember writing down the word *dyslexia* on a 3-by-5 card. I stared at it. What a rotten trick. What a strange word. The difficulty of processing it is almost self-diagnosing. It's difficult to read, virtually impossible to pronounce, and a real pain to spell. I knew it would take me a while to get that word into my brain. I took the card home. The counselor in the Office for the Disabled told me to call Recording for the Blind, because she thought they might be willing to accept me as a trial case and allow me to use their audiobook academic library.

Then she suggested that I contact a psychologist and arrange for an evaluation. Going for that test was the scariest thing I ever did. What if, after the evaluation, I was told, "Sorry, your problem is that you're just not very bright"?

That was not the case. In 1981, at the age of 32, I was diagnosed with severe dyslexia. The psychologist wrote, "Mrs. Tessler named all words quickly and accurately through the middle third-grade level. Her reading speed is far below that which you would expect from an adult. She is highly developed at applied and abstract reasoning acumen when written ability is not involved." He noted that I was coping, thanks to my intelligence and strong problem-solving skills.

With that diagnosis, I qualified for a critical accommodation: I could have the GRE read to me. That's how I took the test, and I scored like a normal graduate student.

I often think about what my life would have been like if I hadn't found out that I was dyslexic, if I hadn't walked through that door. I'm so grateful I did.

...

I applied to the doctoral program again, and I was admitted. I was a doctoral candidate. Let me say that again. *I was a doctoral candidate.*

But still, people doubted me. A nationally respected author and psychologist on Temple's faculty predicted that I wouldn't be able to handle statistics because of my dyslexia. (But as you've learned, dyslexia is a language problem, not a statistics problem!) She wasn't being negative or hostile, she just didn't understand dyslexia. Such prejudices about the competency of people with dyslexia were the prevailing wisdom: If you are a dyslexic reader, you'll never get a doctorate. It will be too challenging.

I had to educate her and the people on the admissions committee about dyslexia. I didn't know it at the time, but this was to be the first of my many campaigns to increase awareness about learning disabilities.

In 1988, I received my doctorate. I was Linda Tessler, Ph.D. *Dr. Linda!* And I blame it all on my mother. Her enthusiasm for learning was contagious.

The "Official" Definition of Dyslexia

In 2002, the Board of Directors of the International Dyslexia Association adopted the official definition of dyslexia:

"Dyslexia is a specific learning disability that is neurological in origin. It is characterized by difficulties with accurate and/or fluent word recognition and poor spelling and decoding abilities. These difficulties typically result from a deficit in the phonological component of language that is often unexpected in relation to other cognitive abilities and the provision of effective classroom instruction. Secondary consequences may include problems in reading comprehension and reduced reading experience that can impede the growth of vocabulary and background knowledge."

This is a good and accurate definition, but it took me years to understand it!

Fueling Up for the Trip

"I couldn't read. I just scraped by. My solution back then was to read classic comic books because I could figure them out from the context of the pictures. Now I listen to books on tape."

- Charles R. Schwab, dyslexic reader and founder and CEO of the Charles Schwab Corporation, the first discount brokerage firm in the nation and a pioneer in the world of online investing.

FINDING MOTIVATION

Finding Motivation

The greater the challenge, the greater the motivation needed to meet it. But where do you find your motivation? How can you develop and harness it?

Some people with learning disabilities act as if they have given up. They seem like they don't care, but the truth is that they do. They desperately want to move away from feelings of failure, criticism and rejection. They often experience limited ability to meet their own – and others' – expectations.

From personal experience, I know that when I catch myself struggling or wanting to quit, it's because I've become fixated on the results, instead of focusing on what I'm doing and accomplishing at the time. I get frustrated because I haven't reached the goal. That's an unproductive distraction.

Here are some ways to find motivation:

Move into a childlike frame of mind:
Adults sometimes develop motivation by getting into a childlike frame of mind. Not childish, childlike – with a sense of awe and wonder. Children learn by playing. Their goal is to have fun. It's important to reconnect with that perspective. If you lose your sense of delight, then you lose your motivation.

Identify your interests:
Your interests are a clue to your strengths. If you're interested in cooking and nutrition, read labels, watch the Food Channel, page through cookbooks, experiment in the kitchen, and invite friends over for special meals. Pursue your interest and read books or trade magazines associated with it. Allow yourself to dream.

My passion was psychology and, fortunately, that's where I also have some aptitude. It's amazing what can happen when you consciously begin to develop your innate strengths, talents and interests: You can have the experience of success.

Use your dreams to create your goal. Dreams are like stars;
even though you may never reach them,
they will help you find your way.

Acknowledge yourself:
Positive reinforcement and empowering self-talk create good feelings. Notice your achievements – every single small step that you accomplish. Learn one new word each day, each week or each month, and then congratulate yourself for learning that word. If you don't acknowledge yourself, you will remain stuck, discouraged and frustrated.

Climbing a mountain provides a useful metaphor about taking – and appreciating – the small steps. At first, just climb to the top of a small hill. At the plateau of the hill, sit down, take a deep breath, enjoy the view and have a picnic. When you're ready, attempt the next hill. If you succeed, great; if you don't, at least you had a picnic.

Learning is self-motivating. Set your own level of achievement and your own expectations. Don't let other people do this for you. The excitement of learning and the pride taken in understanding new things are all sources of self-fulfillment.

Create a safe place in your mind:
Imagine yourself at the beach, in the woods, or maybe in your cozy bed. Go to this emotional retreat whenever it's needed.

Use *everything* as motivation:

I use every argument with my husband as a reminder that I need to be independent, stand on my own two feet, and have a career. Both harmony and disharmony in my family became sources of motivation; harmony offered support, and disharmony underscored the need for self-actualization.

Learn to fail successfully:

At first, this may seem like a contradiction in terms, but make it a point to learn from your failures. They, too, can motivate you to keep trying until you get it right or to change your path to reach your goal.

When you fail, consider it feedback – a caution sign that you are off-course. Learn lessons from your failures, so you don't repeat the actions that prevented you from succeeding.

My mother taught me to note the small accomplishments – as well as the major ones. Along with her unconditional love, that was the greatest single contribution she made to my development of self-esteem.

The difference between success and failure is sometimes merely a point of view: Experts believe that Thomas Alva Edison, inventor of the light bulb, had dyslexia. Edison tried a thousand different materials, including bamboo and cotton, to make a durable filament. A visiting friend saw the results of his experiments and said, "Dr. Edison, give up. You have failed 1000 times."

"I have not failed at all," Edison answered. "I have successfully identified 1000 materials that do not work."

One way to overcome fear of failure is to expose yourself to it so many times that you're no longer concerned about it. After my experiences in school and after failing out of X-ray tech school, I'd had so much practice failing that it empowered me. I was no longer afraid.

Another approach is to have a backup plan. If things don't go the way you want them to, you know what else you can do.

By learning to "fail successfully," you become less reactive to what happens to you and more proactive, so you can reach your destination.

...

You've heard of rose-colored glasses? Think about how your life would change if you lived it wearing success-colored glasses. You'd approach every situation wearing glasses that magnified your *successes* and what you learned from those experiences. When you didn't succeed, your glasses would reveal what it was you needed to learn from that experience. The learning itself would be motivational.

You can handle tremendous adversity if you have self-respect. If things don't go the way you want them to, you'll know that you did your best.

This book focuses on changing what I call your "emotional posture"– how you approach your life emotionally – so that you can motivate yourself. Every therapist has met the popular person who is lonely, the rich person who feels poor, and the smart person who feels stupid. Don't be one of these people. If you are, begin changing. James Taylor said it well when he sang, *"It's enough to be on your way... It's enough to cover ground... It's enough to be moving on..."*

If you can find within yourself a small hint of motivation, keep reading. There is hope!

CHAPTER 21

THE JOYS OF RECORDED TEXT

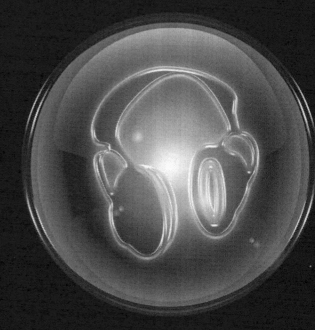

When we listen to a book, we say we are "reading it." It's your ideas and insights that are important, not how you came by them.

The Joys of Recorded Text

If only I hadn't had to wait until I was 32 years old to understand what I had been experiencing! It took me more than three decades to learn that there is nothing diseased or damaged about my brain. Some brains are more effective at reading than others. My brain simply takes a less efficient pathway to interpret words.

For me, the best part of being diagnosed with dyslexia was learning that I could have the printed word – including the Graduate Record Exam and my textbooks – read aloud to me. This one accommodation leveled my playing field, allowing me to perform as well as the other doctoral candidates.

I needed nothing else. My papers were always proofread by Mr. Cooke, who, besides being an English teacher, was a Fulbright Scholar. If he said the grammar was correct, it was correct. Having him help me was like using a jackhammer to crack open an egg.

No teachers or professors ever liked my writing, but I couldn't afford to care. I got my point across. (It strikes me funny that before my doctorate Mr. Cooke was my tutor; afterward he became my editor. The same man was doing the same thing – only the label had changed. That's more evidence that what counts is how you view your circumstances.)

Learning Through Listening

It took me 32 years to find Recording for the Blind, a nonprofit organization created after World War II by Anne Macdonald. She had been inspired by blind veterans who had returned home from the war and wanted to take advantage of the G.I. Bill to further their education. She organized her friends in New York City as her volunteer corps to record books onto vinyl records. In time, the organization would evolve, expand and change its name to Recording for the Blind & Dyslexic (RFB&D). Today, it is known as RFB&D Learning Through Listening.

Recording for the Blind and I were born the same year (1948), but we both needed to grow up first. Educators didn't know what to do with me, and although I didn't know it at the time, help was in the future. I was one of the first dyslexic readers accepted into their program. It was on a trial basis, and I was afraid the trial would end and I would not be able to continue. It was silly of me, but I pretended to be blind when I called to order tapes. That's how much the recordings meant to me. They mobilized me so I could get around in the literate world. They also delighted me.

Imagine that your mind is like a ranch house. Discovering books on tape is like someone adding a 40-story high-rise on top. Suddenly I had so many floors, rooms and windows. There were limitless things to see, limitless perspectives to appreciate. Because of RFB&D, I was able to "read" science, history, art history, psychology, fiction and biography. I could read anything. Whole new worlds opened up to me.

It is no exaggeration to say that RFB&D Learning Through Listening changes lives. I'm living proof. Attaining my doctorate would not have been possible without recorded text. But although recorded text made learning possible, it was still not easy.

In the 1970s, books were recorded onto audiocassettes, which were often hard to hear. It was difficult, if not nearly impossible, to navigate from page to page and from chapter to chapter. But I appreciated what I had, no matter how imperfect.

Today, an army of volunteers has recorded more than 100,000 textbooks, and that number is growing. These volunteers donate a few hours a week to read text aloud at professionally equipped recording studios around the country. They read with emotion, intonation and understanding. Reading monitors and audio engineers are present to ensure the quality of the content and sound. Today, the text is put on CDs. The sound is excellent, there is plenty of volume, and you can navigate forward or backward through the books by simply putting in a page number. The best part is that you get to hear real people reading a story to you. By the end of the book, I would feel like I knew the readers, and I greatly appreciated their collective generosity.

RFB&D's mission is to record all of the country's textbooks. If you need a textbook that hasn't been recorded, you can apply to RFB&D Learning Through Listening. (Borrowers must buy a special player designed for RFB&D recordings in order to honor publishers' copyright laws.)

Earning a doctorate is always going to be a daunting, intense, time-consuming task, but it's much easier today for those with dyslexia than it was in the past.

The High Cost of a Learning Disability

A disproportionate number of juvenile delinquents and people in the penal system have learning disabilities; many of them are unable to read. According to a report by the Philadelphia Unit of RFB&D, 35 percent of students with learning disabilities drop out of school, in contrast to 11 percent of the general student population. Thirty-one percent of these students get in trouble with the law three to five years out of high school. People who can't read get lost in our society; their untapped potential, which can be unleashed through reading, is almost unimaginable. RFB&D Learning Through Listening can make a huge difference for this population.

CHAPTER 25

TIPS FOR USING RECORDED TEXT

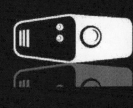

Tips for Using Recorded Text

Don't make the same mistake I made. It takes some time to get used to listening to books read aloud, but what a change it will make in your life once you do.

I have always enjoyed art, yet because of my learning disability, I was cut off from studying art appreciation or art history.

So for my first book, I ordered *Naked Came I*, a biography of French sculptor Auguste Rodin. I was psyched to listen to it.

I recall people talking about what a good book it was, which reminds me of yet another way I had felt left out. I hadn't been able to discuss the books that everyone was reading. No longer. Now, I could jump in. No one thought to ask, "Hey, Linda, did you actually sit down and read the book by flipping through the pages?"

Auguste Rodin died in 1917, but he was reborn for me the day the audiobook arrived in the mail. I took the box of six cassettes and sat down at my kitchen table with a cup of tea. I was trying to slow this moment down, to savor it. I put the first cassette into the tape recorder. I was so excited.

I listened for several hours and then realized something: I was not processing the words. I was hearing them, but I wasn't really getting it. I was getting lost in the story, and I couldn't keep track of the characters, the dates, and the places. I was becoming as *dis*couraged as I had been *en*couraged earlier.

I flat out stopped ordering the tapes. They didn't work. What a huge letdown.

I didn't realize that it was the discouragement, not the speed bump, that was the problem. I didn't give myself time to discover how to match the way I learned with how I should listen to recorded text. Also, I had no one to talk to about my adjustment problem.

Today, listeners get tips on how to take advantage of the technology. You can call RFB&D Learning Through Listening for help.

I continued to struggle with my academic reading requirements. A year later, I found myself in a terribly difficult graduate class. I was really worried about the reading. Out of desperation, I ordered the textbook on tape. This time, I listened while reading along and underlining in the textbook. This turned out to be the key for me: *reading along while listening*. For me, getting auditory, kinesthetic (feeling and doing) and visual modalities into the learning process made a world of difference.

Don't take your first listening experience too seriously, any more than you'd think your first time on a bicycle is the way it's always going to be. You must explore different methods of listening to find the one that works for you.

Here's what works for me: I listen to a simple pleasure book without reading along. If a pleasure book contains many names, dates and places, I listen along with the book beside me so I can see the names in print and circle them to keep the characters and dates straight. The books I want to process deeply, I listen to while reading along. If I really want to know a book, I may listen to it twice. Just as dyslexic readers have trouble remembering certain things, their minds are steel traps for ideas.

It takes longer to listen to a book than it does to read it to yourself. My son Keith and I both find it advantageous to do something else while we are listening to books whose content is not too demanding. When Keith was a little boy, he would play with Legos or draw a picture about whatever book he was listening to. For more information about giving recorded text to children, see Chapter 31.

Today, we both listen while we take a walk or drive a car. I listen while I cook, make beds, straighten closets and clean the house. The player has a speed control that allows me to listen to the recording as quickly or as slowly as I want.

When listening to books read aloud, you need to be an active listener. Sometimes you might get distracted and tune out while the recording continues to play.
The trick is to teach yourself to recognize as early as possible that you are off track and to simply back up the text and repeat. It is a skill you can teach yourself.

Where to Find Audiobooks

Those of us with dyslexia need to be freed from the burden of the word so we can use our rich conceptual abilities. Technology is moving so fast. Go with it. Get the information into your ears however you can. Watch the movie before or after you read the book. Join a study group or book club.

If you have a documented learning disability, subscribe to these services:

Recording for the Blind and Dyslexic (www.rfbd.org, 866-732-3585) offers digitally recorded textbooks on CDs. The books are read aloud by people, not computers, and they are easy to understand. To listen, you currently need a specially adapted CD player or software, which is available through the organization.

Bookshare.org's individual subscriptions enable "all-you-can-read" access to books in easy-to-use digital formats for a full year. Their books and periodicals contain the full text of the publication (not pre-recorded audio) that can be read with the adaptive technology of the reader's choice. A talking software application is included with membership.

The National Library Service for the Blind and Physically Handicapped/NLS (www.loc.gov/nls/, 202-707-5100) offers free audio materials by postage-free mail through the public library system.

Download books from the Internet:

You can download audiobooks from **Apple's iTunes store** (www.apple.com/itunes/store/audiobooks.html). There are tens of thousands of titles, from mysteries to biographies to self-help books. You can listen to them on your computer, your iPod or your iPhone.

LibriVox (http://librivox.org) is striving to make all public domain books available as free audio books; their volunteers record books and put the files back on the Internet.

www.audible.com (888-283-5051) and **www.rightaudiobooks.com** have huge inventories available at a per-book or monthly rate.

Make your computer more user-friendly:

Consider using some text-to-speech software, such as **TextHelp** (www.texthelp.com, 888-248-0652). It reads aloud e-mail, Web pages, reports and more on your computer. TextHelp has been a lifesaver for me. I use it every time I sit down at my computer.

With advanced optical character recognition technology, **Kurzeil 3000** (www.kurzweiledu.com, 800-894-5374) allows you to scan a printed page. It can read that page to you, along with word-processed documents, e-mail and Web pages.

CHAPTER 26

TIME FOR ME TO GIVE BACK

If you're tired of reading, you can skip this section. When you are able to, make a point of giving back to others in your own way and at your own time. It creates a deep sense of satisfaction, happiness and self-esteem.

Time for Me to Give Back

After I received my doctorate, I became a Recording for the Blind volunteer, serving on their board in Philadelphia and on the National Advisory Board. I was no longer afraid of being kicked out. I was no longer worried that I would be demobilized.

Our goal was to develop an infrastructure to help Recording for the Blind expand and evolve so it could support the population with dyslexia. To do that, we needed to get funding from the federal government. I was extremely honored to be asked to testify before the Appropriations Committee of the House of Representatives in Washington, D.C., in the hopes of raising money for the project.

In 1995, the organization officially changed its name to Recording for the Blind & Dyslexic (RFB&D). We created an outreach program to make people aware of our services. Tears of joy came to my eyes when I became part of a committee to help put recorded texts into the classroom. If only I had been one of those children who could turn on a player and have my science, social studies or history read to me. I still would have gotten a "D" in reading, but I wouldn't have been cut off from the other subjects.

I often think about my mother and my Uncle Freddy, who lived their entire lives with undiagnosed dyslexia, without access to accommodations. Both struggled in school, never reaching their intellectual potential. My mother graduated from high school. My Uncle Freddy didn't, although he later received a high school equivalency degree.

My mother never pursued a career, although she longed to. But she proved her competence in many other ways: she served on boards, was a political committeewoman, and she ran hugely successful fundraising operations for Hahnemann University Hospital. Still, she felt unfulfilled and burdened by her dyslexia. Although she was able to read, she didn't feel good about herself. She was embarrassed.

There remains a great need to make people with print disabilities (those who can't effectively read standard print because of a disability) aware of the extensive services that exist for them.

...

My life's work has been to increase the awareness of learning disabilities and to let the volunteers and staff at RFB&D Learning Through Listening know how tremendously I appreciate them. When I listen, it seems as if they are reading just to me. I feel connected to them. These people, along with Dr. Mathern and Mr. Cooke, are angels in my life.

After I interviewed Bruce Jenner for my dissertation and told him about RFB&D, he joined their national council.
I'm still a member. Using recorded text is a way of life for me.

I remember feeling badly for the poor volunteers who read my upper level statistics to me. What an arduous task that must have been, but they did it for me anyway. I have met some of the volunteers and asked them why they do it. Most want to help create a better world and, through RFB&D, they do, because the borrowers who use their recordings contribute much more to the world as a result. The greatest tribute to the organization is what people who use their "learning through listening" services make of themselves.

The publishers of these books have also been extremely generous in allowing them to be recorded. Their gift has not been acknowledged enough. I send my heartfelt gratitude to them.

I have a great deal to give back because of what has been given to me. If you are interested, please climb aboard to help us move forward.

"I am only one, but still, I am one. I cannot do everything, but I can do something. And, because I cannot do everything, I will not refuse to do what I can." - Edward Everett Hale

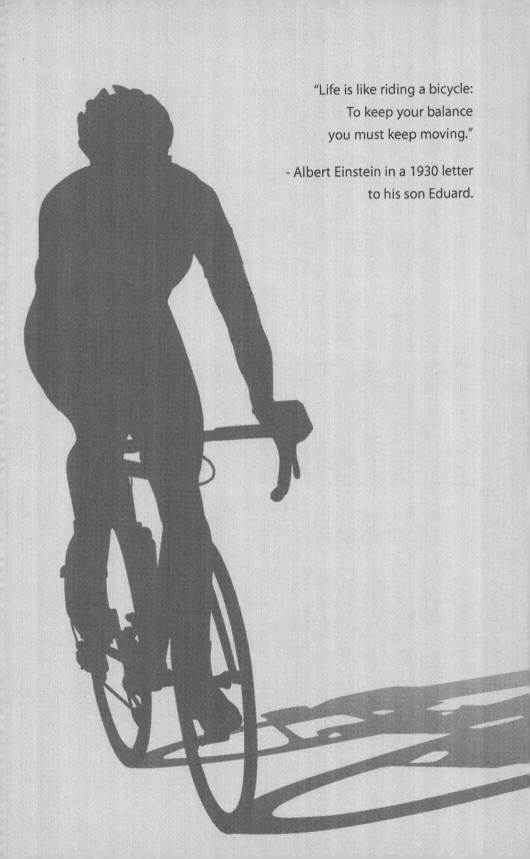

"Life is like riding a bicycle:
To keep your balance
you must keep moving."

- Albert Einstein in a 1930 letter
to his son Eduard.

Mapping Out
a Road to Success

"It doesn't matter how or even when I learn something, because once I have learned it, I have it forever and it seems as though the knowledge was always there."

– Dr. Florence P. Haseltine, a dyslexic reader who went on to become a Reproductive Endocrinologist and Director of the Center for Population Research at the National Institutes of Health

CHAPTER 27

THE SIX CLUES

The Six Clues to Successfully Managing a Learning Disability

If you have gotten this far, congratulations. I've saved the best for last. The following chapters bring all of these ideas together, so that when you finish reading the book, you'll have some useful tools to take with you on your journey.

No one has ever developed character without struggle, and learning disabilities present many opportunities for character development. Struggling with it can teach us essential life lessons. This is one of the many gifts of dyslexia.

In the chapters that follow, I've laid out the psychological strategies – or "Six Clues" — that I used to help manage my life with dyslexia. These clues are not a quick fix. They are a road map for dealing with the challenges presented by any learning difference and for achieving success in all endeavors.

The strategies are discussed in much greater depth in books such as Benjamin Franklin's *The Way To Wealth*, Napoleon Hill's *Think and Grow Rich*, Zig Ziglar's *See You at the Top*, Steven Covey's *The 7 Habits of Highly Successful People*, and Anthony Robbins' *Unlimited Power*, among many others. These books are success-literature classics, well worth checking out.

Through the years, many articles about dyslexia have presented its negative manifestations, pathology, and the resulting emotional distress. Only a handful have addressed the processes that successful people use to overcome a learning disability. In other words, weaknesses were spelled out clearly, while strengths essentially went unexplored.

To create a productive, satisfying life, we must study and maximize productive thoughts and behaviors. Remember that learning disabilities cannot only be managed, but they can also be a real tool in helping us learn how to achieve success.

Here's my definition of success: Success is not about accumulating material things, but you do have to make a living. Success is feeling fulfilled. Success is getting to do what you love to do. Success is having meaningful relationships throughout your life. Success is living life to the fullest and being at peace with yourself.

How to Use the Six Clues

THE SIX CLUES TO SUCCESSFULLY MANAGING A LEARNING DISABILITY

❑ TAKE ACTION

❑ PRIORITIZE AND PACE YOURSELF

❑ SET UP A SUPPORT SYSTEM

❑ LOOK INSIDE AND LIKE WHAT YOU SEE

❑ CREATE BALANCE

❑ MATCH YOUR GOALS TO YOUR STRENGTHS

Consider the Six Clues slowly, one idea at a time. See what rings true to you. Make notes about the ideas you want to implement. You can do this on pages 18 and 19. If you haven't dog-eared them yet, please do so now, so you can easily refer to your notes.

Absorb, expand and develop the ideas that work for you. Then act on them. It's not good enough to just think about and understand an idea. If you don't change the habit or pattern, you have not done the work. Take advantage of the realizations you make as you read this book. They are gifts of awareness that may not come again. This is life-changing work.

Finally, don't read this section just once and put it away. Put a list of the Six Clues on your refrigerator, on your desk, and in your wallet. In the future, when you encounter a roadblock in your path, refer to the Six Clues. Surely one of them will help you get back on the right path.

Clue #1:

TAKE ACTION

Then keep moving. When you stay in motion, the world presents options to you.

You've found out that you have a learning disability. Go ahead and grieve. It's part of the normal healing process – as long as it is only a first step and not a permanent condition.

You may also be relieved to finally have a name for what you've been experiencing, to have information, and to know that you are not alone. Whatever you feel is exactly what you should feel. There is no correct way to react.

Put your learning disability in perspective. It's part of who you are – not the sum total of you. Understand that you have a learning difference, which gives you some advantages and some disadvantages. You will have to work hard, but life is not easy for anyone. Learning disabilities can be managed.

It's helpful to think of your imperfections in the same way we regard handmade objects. Such items are cherished precisely for their imperfections. The human touch, with all its imperfections, makes an item unique and valuable. Regard yourself in the same generous way.

Next, take – and stay – in action. Don't allow yourself to sit around and mope, wring your hands, or sink into despondency. Your learning disability needs attention!

Question. Investigate. Research. Pick the brain of someone with a similar problem. Ask questions to identify the help that's available to you. Contact any or all of the following nonprofit organizations that are involved in education and advocacy for those with learning disabilities:

- **The International Dyslexia Association**:
  www.interdys.org or 410-296-0232

- **Learning Disabilities Association of America**:
  www.ldanatl.org or 412-341-1515

- **National Center for Learning Disabilities**:
  www.ncld.org or 212-545-7510

- **RFB&D Learning Through Listening**
  www.rfbd.org or 1-866-732-3585

For a wealth of information, check out LD Online (www.ldonline.org), a comprehensive Web site on learning disabilities and ADHD. It has helpful articles, first-person essays, forums, a list of resources, and a directory of professionals.

It goes without saying that you should get as much remediation as you can. Contact any of the organizations above, your school system, a private reading specialist, or a psychologist who specializes in learning disabilities to find out what your options are. Once you've chosen a remediation plan, set a goal and go for it. Give it some time – a few months, a semester – and then evaluate the plan to see if you are making progress. You might need to try another approach.

Parents, please note there is a direct correlation between early intervention and reading ability. With children, the earlier the diagnosis and remediation, the greater their reading achievement will be.

Dana Blackhurst, an educator and a dyslexic reader, offers this advice: "Once you've hired a tutor or teacher or situated your child in a special school, let the professionals do their job. Empower them. That doesn't mean you shouldn't evaluate the program or the process to make sure it's right, but give it some time – three months, a semester, etc."

Taking action begins by setting a goal for yourself. Then consider the potential negative consequences if you don't achieve it. For example, I thought about what could happen if I were to flunk out of my doctoral program. I decided I could live with the consequences, and so I was able to move forward. I knew that when I was an old woman, I would respect myself more if I tried and failed than if I never tried at all.

To get started, don't look too far ahead or you may be overwhelmed. Break down your big goal into manageable steps that are in your control. For example, "I want to complete a particular course of study" and "I want to earn a certain grade" are not useful goals. The first goal looks too far ahead. The second is out of your control. Even the best students can't fully control the grades their teachers give them. What is in your power, however, is how much you study and use the help that's available to you. You *could* set a goal to spend a specified amount of time each day studying for the course.

Determine the first step to take on the path to your goal. Promise yourself you're going to stick with this first step until it's done, and keep this promise. Self-esteem comes from keeping promises to yourself, from being trustworthy.

When you've completed the first step, evaluate your decision to go down this path. It's okay to change your mind and choose a different path, but if you still want to pursue this goal, get started on the next step.

Achievement, satisfaction and self-fulfillment come from completing each step and knowing that you did your best – not more than your best. Don't obsess, overdo or overreact. Work hard, do want you can do, and then let it go. It's enough to be on your way.

Expect failures and disappointments along the way. The only way to grow is to take chances, to push yourself. You'll never know how much you can achieve if you don't challenge yourself by taking risks. Most great inventors have said that they learned much more from their failures en route to their discoveries than they learned from their successes. Setbacks are a fundamental part of achievement. The people who experience the most failure in their lives are often the most successful.

Regard each disappointment as an opportunity to learn. When you make a mistake, it's one obstacle out of the way. You probably won't make the same error again. And if you do repeat the mistake, don't worry. You obviously needed to!

To Do

When you wake up each morning, identify one thing you want to do that day, such as call a university to ask for an application or review your biology notes. It could even be to learn a new word, which you can put on a 3x5 card and memorize throughout the day.

At the end of each day, check in to identify one step you took to achieve your goal. Even if it's something minor, congratulate yourself on one little victory every day. Make a note of each success – either in your memory or perhaps by putting a star on your calendar. Be your own cheerleader.

Get into the habit of being with words each day – reading, listening, and studying. You won't necessarily enjoy all the reading required to become a better reader, but you will enjoy moving ahead by learning one idea and one word at a time.

Clue #2:

PRIORITIZE AND PACE YOURSELF

Since everything seems to take us longer, we must be skilled at managing our time and our lives.

It's a fact of life that your learning difference slows you down. Yet life moves along at a very fast clip, and you are expected to keep up. Teachers, parents, friends, employers and co-workers will have the same expectations of you as they do of everyone else.

How can you possibly get everything done? The simple answer is: You can't. Once you let it sink in that there is too much to do, stay calm.

Prioritizing will buy you a lot of time. Focus on what's most important. In doing this, you are just like everyone else. No one knows everything about a subject; that would be impossible. Like everyone else, you'll have to learn to identify what is essential for you to study and absorb. You might want to work with a professional psychologist or coach, who can teach you how to zero in on the essentials.

Many people with dyslexia become specialists in one technical field. In part, this is because they can master the relevant vocabulary, freeing them to do the critical thinking for which they have a talent.

"You can do anything. But you can't do everything." No one knows who first said this adage, but it's often touted as good advice. I agree.

You can maximize your time by sorting out what you can do and what you need others to do for you. Successful adults with learning differences frequently hire someone – a typist, proofreader, office manager, administrative assistant, etc. – to do what they cannot do.

To pace yourself, you'll have to define what "keeping up" means to you.

It's a comfort to know that there is no correlation between how long it takes to learn something and how well it is learned. The person who takes five or six years to earn a college degree can be as well educated as the person who does it in four.

Learning enough English may seem impossible, but life is long and the English language is finite. You can learn enough to get by, and your knowledge will increase as you age. You may never be the best speller or a great reader, but you can improve your skills. With practice and experience, you can improve at even the most challenging tasks.

Taking a break is as important an "action" as every forward step. Take time off when you start feeling bogged down or discouraged. Depending on the situation, a break may be an hour, a day or a year. The important thing is to regard it as "time off," not as "the end." Spending time with my family or friends, or sometimes just being alone, has helped me survive.

You will be able to return to the task refreshed and ready to tackle problems, or you may need someone to help you over a hump. Whatever happens, make sure the break is part of your forward motion.

Consciously remind yourself to relax and to take your time. It makes a big difference. Accept your learning pace as your personal style.

To Do

These four principles will help you prioritize and pace yourself.

1. Get organized. Disorganization costs time and increases stress. Since it's overwhelming to tackle all aspects of disorganization at once, work on one problem area at a time. For example, if your bedroom is messy, start organizing one corner. Remember to congratulate yourself when it's done. Develop a system of organization that you can maintain. (For many individuals with a learning difference, organization can only be achieved with a professional coach.)

2. Be aware of your daily high- and low-energy periods. As much as possible, do your hardest tasks first during your high-energy hours. I work first thing in the morning or late at night.

3. Do what you are *more* likely to do – after you do what you are least likely to do. For example, do homework before watching television. Always use the adage "Worst first."

4. Get into the habit of finishing the task at hand. Much of the time, you'd probably rather be doing something else. Someone said, "Anything worth doing isn't easy."

You might want to put the book down to do this work now. Then, go on to the next clue. You can do the same after each clue. That way, you can think about how to apply the ideas to your life.

Slow down. The only thing that you should be in a rush to do is to make changes that will improve your life.

Clue #3:

SET UP A SUPPORT SYSTEM

Modern technology can free us from many difficulties imposed by our learning style. A social support system can empower us.

You have no idea how much you can accomplish once you fully

accept the fact that you need help. It's okay – even necessary – to accept help. In fact, you must do so in order to free up the talent you have.

It takes a strong person to acknowledge weaknesses and ask for help. Many dyslexic people have trouble doing this. If this describes you, just do it anyway. The more you ask for help, the more comfortable you will become. You can't wait until it *feels* comfortable.

Building and maintaining a reliable support system is essential for success. That support system should be two-tiered.

Your technical support system includes the technology that makes life and learning manageable, such as a digital voice recorder to record a lecture and a computer that reads aloud. A personal digital assistant (PDA) and a calculator are also invaluable aids. By my bedside, where I do my reading, I keep a Merriam-Webster Speaking Dictionary & Thesaurus, a hand-held electronic device made by Franklin Electronic Publishers. I type in a word I want to know, push a button, and it says the word. That's a great help.

Also, you'll need numerous and reliable sources for recorded text, such as Recording for the Blind & Dyslexic, the National Library Service for the Blind and Physically Handicapped, and your local library and bookstore. Get a CD player or an iPod so that you can download books from the Internet.

Technical support also includes the people who teach you and help you with various tasks. Your technical support team may include a coach, tutor, reader, editor, spell-checker, typist, and computer assistant, among others. These individuals must contribute to your sense of self-esteem without undermining it. You can tell they are trustworthy people because you feel safe around them.

You need a backup for your support system, such as a second tech support person who you can call if the first one isn't available. Renowned race car driver Jackie Stewart said that from struggling with his dyslexia, he learned to be "a belt and suspenders person" – an attitude that helped him win three Formula One world titles.

The second tier, and equally as important, is your **social support system.** The role of family members in your support system is critical and difficult. Their instinct is to protect you from pain, make life easier, solve problems, and smooth over rough spots. But, in truth, you're more empowered when you are supported rather than protected.

Family members must learn how to provide *quality* support, which I define as listening without saying too much. Quality support means that your family validates your difficulties, but allows you to assume the role of doer, problem solver, independent thinker and self-reliant individual. People with dyslexia must assume all of these roles to reach their potential.

Social support also includes friends: people who accept you for who you are, people with whom you can be yourself. Create a social support system that will travel with you on your journey. Create partnerships of complimentary talents.

To Do

When was the last time you consciously set about to make a friend? It's probably been a long time. It might be time to do so in order to grow your social support network. Here's a guide.

1. Look around and decide who you want to befriend. Hint: Observe how someone treats others in order to make a good guess as to how they will treat you.

2. Get to know that person better by making a plan to get together. You could invite him or her out to lunch or to your home.

Pretend you are playing baseball. If they don't respond three times, then it's three strikes and you're out. Don't contact them again. But don't take it personally; we're all way too busy.

Likewise, if someone invites you over for dinner or makes the first overture, reciprocate (if you want to establish a friendship). Reciprocating is a way to make a friend.

3. If the relationship seems to have a "green light," call or visit periodically. Find the rhythm that works for the two of you. It can be once a week or once a month. You don't need to be on a rigid schedule, but be sure to call again. On the other hand, calling too much can be a problem.

4. Keep a notation of your friend's birthday, anniversary and other special occasions. Call or send a card. Be sure to be there for the difficult times, too, – an illness, hospital stay, or death of a loved one.

5. Do not judge. Love, accept and seek to understand your friend. Never talk about someone behind his or her back.

6. When you're feeling comfortable, start sharing personal feelings with each other. When you do that, you will become closer and feel safer.

7. Help your friend and give him or her the gift of helping you in return. People want to make a difference.

Clue #4:

LOOK INSIDE AND LIKE WHAT YOU SEE

Self-respect is "inside" work. Throughout our lives, there will be many chances to boost our emotional intelligence.

You've established a reliable support system. You've set up achievable goals. You're working hard, and things are going well.

Then you start looking ahead, and the end seems too far away. You don't think you can sustain the level of effort needed to go on, or you come across what seems to be an insurmountable problem. You think about giving up.

Don't get caught in this trap. Everyone gets discouraged at times. It's a symptom of life, not of a learning disability. Those who have learning issues must judge themselves by appropriate standards. This doesn't mean lesser standards; it means different standards.

> *You can't change how your brain processes information, but you can choose how you feel about it. Appreciate the positive side of the way your mind works.*

I once counseled a medical student who was successfully coping with his dyslexia by using the available accommodations. He had a well-formed learning strategy that took advantage of all of his sensory modalities (seeing, hearing, and doing) to reinforce the learning. It allowed him to retain the most information and have the best comprehension.

He wanted to shorten his learning process. It was a fair goal, but I couldn't help him. The truth is that every successful person I interviewed for my dissertation had to work harder – and slower – than his or her peers to accomplish the very same tasks.

What I *could* give that medical student was a greater acceptance of his learning style. In psychology, this is called a "reframe." This freed up his energy because he was not upset with himself anymore.

The happiest people are those who stay focused on their *own* game plan and measure today's success against yesterday's. Delayed gratification is an essential part of a successful life.

If you do fall into the trap of discouragement, positive reinforcement and positive thinking can help you get out. First, become conscious of what has gone well. For the moment, ignore the things you don't like; they will only discourage you. Focusing on what's wrong is a common – and huge – mistake.

Your self-image is in your control. You can turn your anger and frustration into determination and motivation.

A key to self-esteem is what you say to yourself. Develop the habit of being conscious of your inner voice. Do you say respectful, kind and constructive things to yourself? If a negative thought comes up, do you respond with calming, sympathetic statements, or do you let the thought disturb your peace of mind? Unpleasant thoughts pop into all of our heads. Just be sure to answer that negative thought with a positive one.

Dissatisfaction often arises when you compare yourself to others. Don't do it. Your goals and achievements are unique to you and shouldn't be measured against anyone else's.

Reality Check: Life is a little empty and lonely at times for everyone. We think we are not enough, but we are more than enough.

To Do

Here are a few insights designed to help you maintain a winning self-image:

• Notice small improvements and pat yourself on the back for them. Learn to feel satisfaction from every step forward.

• Make promises to yourself and keep them. If you tell yourself, "I'm going to read a chapter every night," then do it. A winning self-image depends on honoring your promises.

• View problems and obstacles as feedback, never as failure. Road blocks are just signals telling you that you may need to do things differently. Try a different road to get to the same place, but keep moving. You will find something that works.

• Find ways to soothe yourself when things are not going well. A natural reaction to problems is to hurry through in order to get past the stressful situation. For the person with a learning disability, this is a disaster. Actually, it's a disaster for anyone. At stressful times, you must stay true to your rhythm and slow down more than usual. Literally, stop to breathe slowly and deeply. Relax yourself back to what you were doing.

• You need to take breaks and, at times, a lot of breaks. Take time to talk to a support person, or do something physical, such as running, playing ball, or taking a walk. Yoga and meditation are good stress-reducers for some people.

• Develop some talent. Your talent doesn't have to be natural gift, such as that of an athlete, musician or dancer. It could be something you enjoy and that gives you a sense of accomplishment: craft projects, an after-school job, or a million other things. When actress Lindsay Wagner, TV's first Bionic Woman, was having trouble in school because of her dyslexia, she became the best babysitter in town; she would create puppet shows for the children.

• A sense of humor helps smooth the way. Laughter is the lubricant for life. Apply freely.

Clue #5:

✓ CREATE BALANCE

The old adage about not putting all of your eggs in one basket is true and will allow you to handle the inevitable setbacks.

When managing your dyslexia or managing your life, it's easy to focus intently on one aspect and lose track of the bigger picture. In fact, many people focus so completely that they simply forget to live their lives.

There is something specific you can do – and that's to consciously create balance in your life. You need to eat well, exercise, develop hobbies, feel passionate about things, spend time with friends, keep appointments, and just live life. You must make time to nourish your physical, mental, emotional and spiritual self. Make sure your daily habits support you.

Individuals with learning differences must also strike a balance on the frustration tightrope. Frustration is a motivator when it inspires you to work hard, find new ways to solve problems, and handle difficult situations. On the other hand, if you encounter too much frustration, you're bound to give up. You must find the level of frustration that spurs you on to challenge yourself.

To Do

Review how you spend your time by analyzing your calendar.

1. With a black pencil, underline anything you did that turned out to be a waste of time.

2. With a blue pencil, underline any activity you did that you could have delegated to someone else. (If someone else can do the job 75-80 percent as well, delegate it.)

3. In red, underline anything you did that contributes to your physical and mental health.

4. Use green (it symbolizes growth) to underline anything you did to help yourself, others, or the world in general, or anything you did that involved learning.

5. Finally, get a highlighter in your favorite color and highlight anything you did with family, friends or just for fun.

Clue #6:

✔ MATCH YOUR GOALS TO YOUR STRENGTHS

Make a match between your strengths, talents and goals. Do not build a life on your weaknesses. You need to manage them. This clue is vitally important.

Dealing effectively with a learning disability means developing your strengths and managing your weaknesses. It means choosing a profession in which your strengths can be brought into play and your weaknesses can be accommodated.

Dyslexic people can work in a myriad of occupations. Nothing is off limits, but you may need to find someone to help you with the language aspect. While doing research for my doctoral dissertation, I interviewed a United States senator, an educator, two actors, a playwright, an Olympic decathlon champion, a race car driver, and the publisher of *The New York Times*. I even spoke with a world-renowned brain researcher.

All of these people chose a vocation that relied on their strengths. All had support staff around them to help manage their weaknesses.

Talents come so easily to people that we frequently don't even recognize them. How do you find your talents? Look at your passions. What do you yearn to do? What's satisfying? If you discover a spark, continue down that road. A spark is a green light that tells you to keep moving.

Note to parents: Exposing children to as many varied academic, artistic and athletic pursuits as possible increases the probability of their discovering a passion.

What do you learn quickly? What are you good at? Many individuals with LD become experts in a highly specialized field, which means they have a limited number of words to master.

Ben Franklin considered it a tragedy not to use one's strengths. He compared it with a sundial placed in the shade. Don't define yourself or let anyone else define you by your weaknesses.

My going to X-ray tech school was a perfect example of not using Clue #6. I did not make a match that suited my strengths. Neither did one of my clients, who was working as an administrative assistant, a job that required her to send a lot of correspondence. She struggled with spelling and grammar, and she was unhappy. However, she was terrific at planning things. She quit her job, and today she is a successful event planner.

Clue #6 is the hardest one to implement, because many people with learning disabilities have never been taught to focus on their strengths. Your life will not work until you apply this last clue.

To Do

From this day on, think about what you are good at and build a career around those talents. To get started, consider the following categories and make a few notes about each one.

Your personality: Do you enjoy being with people or do you prefer to be alone? Are you shy or outgoing? Analytical or artistic? If you're shy, you probably wouldn't be happy as a salesperson; if you're outgoing, you might not want to work alone at a computer all day.

Your interests: What do you like to do? What do you enjoy watching on television, reading about or discussing?

Your aptitude: What are you good at? You might love airplanes, but if you're not a good mathematician, aeronautical engineering might not be the best field for you.

Your values: How much do you want to earn? How many hours a week do you want to work? How long a distance are you willing to commute?

An excellent book to read on this topic is *Now, Discover your Strengths* by Marcus Buckingham and Donald Clifton, Ph.D. You could also meet with a vocational counselor, who will give you exercises to explore these four areas and help you identify suitable options.

…

These, then, are the Six Clues to Successfully Managing a Learning Disability. Respecting and embracing these ideas can change your life. We can't change the core of who we are, but we can change our thinking, our behavior, our values, and how we perceive and respond to situations. We can learn skills and gain knowledge.

I know that advice is easy to give and hard to live, but just try this: Do what you can, and then do a little more. It's all about imagining how you are going to feel – and what you are going to do – after you accomplish your goals. Carry that image with you.

CHAPTER
28

SWEET REVENGE

Sweet Revenge

After I earned my doctorate, I decided to take a year-long postgraduate course to deepen my therapy skills. During the course, we would learn to analyze how individuals process their life experiences. We'd use this information to gain deeper insight into the human mind, increase our rapport with clients, and tailor our therapeutic intervention to fit their processing style. The goal was to make us better therapists.

Midway through the course, I had lunch with a few of my classmates, including a man named Vinnie. He teased me about how I process information. He implied that my kinesthetic approach – based largely on emotional perceptions and doing – would not allow me to learn the material well enough to pass the course. "How are you going to process the information using all those *feelings*?" he joked. He thought that his sequential, auditory learning style was superior and would help him absorb detailed, complex information.

This was a pass or fail course, and the professors determined our fate based on the final exam and nothing else. For the exam, we did therapy with one client. We had to determine the client's processing style and report how we customized our approach to fit that style.

I remember sitting in class on a Friday afternoon, some time after we had all submitted our reports. The professor announced that only one of us had passed the course. The rest would have to repeat the final exam process the following week.

You can guess that I was sure I was among the students who would be repeating the exam. All the others had advanced degrees, and I assumed they were better learners than I, even though I had all of my accommodations in place.

At the end of the class, the professor looked at his watch and said, "Okay, class is over. Have a great weekend." He hadn't announced the test results.

We gathered our books and papers and stood up. Had we missed something? We didn't know who the successful student was.

The professor stood up from his desk. "I'll see everyone back here Monday. Except Linda."

As we were filing out of the classroom, most of the other students congratulated me. I overheard Vinnie's buddy say to him, "And we teased *her* all year!" Vinnie was trying to exit as quickly as he could.

He reluctantly stopped and turned to me. I flashed him a grin and shrugged my shoulders.

I hope he had a great weekend. I did.

Child on Board:
Directions for Parenting

"The popular idea that a child forgets easily is not an accurate one. Many people go right through life in the grip of an idea which has been impressed on them in very tender years."

- Agatha Christie, a British crime fiction writer who, despite her dyslexia, wrote 80 detective novels and many theater plays.

CHAPTER 29

TAKING YOUR CHILD ON THE TRIP

Taking Your Child on the Trip

There is a hereditary component to dyslexia, so if you are reading this book for yourself, it is possible that you may someday have a child with a learning disability. Also, you may realize that a niece or nephew has been struggling, and this information will be useful. If this information doesn't apply now, put it aside for the future, and proceed to the section entitled Almost There, Then a Rock Slide.

When I was a child, whenever something interesting would come up, my mom and I would run, not walk, to the *World Book Encyclopedia* to look it up and read about it. My mom's joy of learning was contagious and carried me through. This love of learning, instilled in me very early in life, will stay with me forever.

"No one works harder at learning than a curious child."
– from **The World Is Flat** *by Thomas L. Friedman*

Parents have two important tasks: to instill in their child a love of learning and to observe their child's progress. As early as ages 3, 4 or 5, children can have rapid naming problems, sometimes evident in the speed at which they say their colors. If you think your child may be at risk – if parents or siblings have a learning disability – it's a good idea to have him or her screened by an early intervention reading teacher. Today, there is so much professional help available for children with learning issues, and the International Dyslexia Association (www.interdys.org) is a great place to go for referrals.

Research shows that with early intervention – before age 7 – the hardwiring of the brain can be changed. With certain types of training, we can trigger the more efficient part of the brain to read. As a result, many children are able to significantly improve their reading, which often means they also learn to enjoy it.

At home, you can read Dr. Seuss, whose rhyming words and vowel sounds are great for children. Because my son and I have dyslexia, I'm concerned that my grandchildren may be at risk. I've made a game of saying vowel sounds with them. These are the hardest sounds to get.

...

Naturally, parents want their children to feel good about themselves, but achieving this is more complicated than it appears. Unfortunately, there are no black and white answers to most problems. In fact, in psychology, all or nothing thinking is considered "thought distortion." The keys to empowering and motivating a child reside in the gray areas.

Guard the Child's Self-image

A poor self-image is a severe handicap. Children are impressionable, and they believe what you tell them. If you call a child "stupid" even in jest, the child will likely take it to heart and carry that belief with him for the rest of his life. Casual remarks such as, "What do you mean you can't find the ketchup? It's in the refrigerator, stupid!" do damage. Name-calling is verbal abuse and it is very, very damaging. *Never do it!*

On the other hand, too much praise can make children feel insecure, because inside they know it's unwarranted. They may think that their parents don't really know them or are trying to fool them. A child should be praised for a specific action: for example, a kindness done to another or a chore that was completed. I call this "deserved praise."

Letting children figure out that they are smart makes more impact than telling them directly. Students who have been told too often that they are bright might believe that if they try and fail, it will prove that they are not so intelligent after all, so they simply don't try.

It is powerful to tell your child, "What a great idea you have. I want to think about that one!"

A Book Series That Builds Self-Esteem

Henry Winkler, who himself struggled with dyslexia, has co-authored a best-selling series of children's books (for ages 8-12) featuring learning-challenged fourth-grader Hank Zipzer, the "world's greatest underachiever." Titles include **Help! Somebody Get Me Out of Fourth Grade** *and* **I Got a D in Salami**.

In an online review of **Summer School! What Genius Thought That Up?** *teacher Ethel Smith wrote, "Henry Winkler and Lin Oliver have nailed the world of the LD child. Hank Zipzer is the quintessential kid with a learning disability. He's smart, he's funny, he thinks outside the box (ok he doesn't even see the box), and he views the world as only a child with LD can. I read this book to my fourth graders who immediately demanded more of the same. Everyone in my class felt an instant kinship to Hank, and gained insight into LD that I could only wish for before. My students with LD identified with Hank and suddenly saw themselves in a different, more positive light."*

Avoid the Extremes of Overinvolvement or Detachment

Family therapy makes useful distinctions between overinvolved parenting and detached parenting. Both extremes should be avoided. Understanding where these extremes lie will help you find the middle of the road.

These definitions will need to be adjusted according to the child's developmental age. In grade school, children need parents to serve as their advocate. When a parent assumes responsibility for the learning struggles of a college student, that's overinvolvement. An evolution to independence must occur during the passage from childhood to adulthood.

You can assist your children, but be careful not to deprive them of the true satisfaction and deep sense of joy that come from overcoming life's problems themselves.

My mother had an indomitable spirit that gave me a positive outlook on the world. She didn't become overly involved in my learning struggle because she couldn't. She herself had learning problems. My father couldn't help me because he was working day and night to support our family.

Overinvolved parents will identify too strongly with their children's struggle. These parents unknowingly try to satisfy their own unmet childhood needs by creating a situation in which they feel needed. Unfortunately, this sends a message that children are unable to solve their own problems or handle their negative emotions. Overinvolved parents unwittingly create a dependent, insecure and unmotivated child. Although parents may believe they are acting out of love for the child, it's one of the most crippling things they can do.

Many individuals who become addicted to drugs were raised by families who overprotected them from the vicissitudes of life. When parents are no longer available to fix every problem and soothe all the pain, and when children, now young adults, don't have the skills needed to deal with their problems, they may turn to drugs.

Detached parents are emotionally distant. They may deny that their child is suffering in school and may even deny that a learning disability exists. In this way, they protect themselves from the pain they would experience if they were to empathize with their child.

In the overinvolved relationship, the boundaries between parent and child are blurred: It's hard to tell where one ends and the other begins. These parents are meeting their own needs through their children, and their children's search for identity is seriously compromised. In the detached relationship, the distance between parent and child is too great. Children may feel isolated and hopeless because it seems that no one is available to help them learn.

When observing parenting patterns, we almost never encounter these extremes. Instead, families lie somewhere along the continuum. The tricky part is that the balance keeps shifting.

Parents can disengage from one of their children while becoming overinvolved with another. A parent may give a child adequate space to deal with social relationships but be overbearing with schoolwork. Relationships need to keep changing as the child matures.

To make good decisions, parents must try to be aware of their own needs and bear in mind that it is not their children's job to fulfill them.

There is hardly a person alive who has no unfulfilled needs. We all hunger for security, love, acceptance and strength, but decisions must be made with a view toward what is best for the child – not the parent. These decisions often feel uncomfortable for the parent, who is reluctant to let go, but they allow the child to grow into adulthood.

In conclusion, we need to find a balance. Sometimes that means giving constructive criticism; other times it means lending support. Parents need to advocate for their kids, but not in an overbearing way. It's best to partner with the teacher or tutor. There is a difference between "love" and "enmeshment." Once that vitally important distinction is understood, you'll understand why I say, "Fortunately I had to own my own problem and do something about it myself."

Powerful Memoirs From Famous Mothers

These three books can help empower parents and let them know that others understand what they are going through.

...

Laughing Allegra: The Inspiring Story of a Mother's Struggle and Triumph Raising a Daughter With Learning Disabilities

Anne Ford, the great granddaughter of Henry Ford and longtime chair of the National Center for Learning Disabilities, wrote this honest and insightful book about her daughter and how learning disabilities shape the lives of the entire family.

...

On Their Own: Creating an Independent Future for Your Adult Child with Learning Disabilities and ADHD: A Family Guide

In her follow-up book, Ford shares the wisdom of her personal experience. It is a hands-on, practical guide for parents of adult children with learning disabilities.

...

A Special Education: One Family's Journey through the Maze of Learning Disabilities

Fashion Designer Dana Buchman's candid memoir reveals her daughter's struggle with learning disabilities and her steep learning curve to become the mother her daughter needed her to be.

CHAPTER 30

TRAVELING DOWN THE MIDDLE OF THE ROAD

Traveling Down
the Middle of the Road

A nurturing parent believes in a child's potential and says encouraging words like "Maybe you can't do this today, but I'll bet you will be able to do it soon" or "I'll bet you can concentrate on your homework for 10 more minutes." Ask toddlers if they want help with a task, such as dressing; ask grade-schoolers if they want help with their homework. If children accept the help, the trick is to give them enough support to get them over the hurdle without actually doing the work for them.

"The greatest injustice against dyslexics is that not enough
is expected of them and that dyslexia is allowed
to be used as an excuse for bad behavior."
– Dr. Charles Drake, founder of Landmark College

Nurturing parents look for things that children can do for themselves and then let them do it. Self-determination and self-mastery instill an invaluable feeling of control, which breeds happiness. On the other hand, children who feel dependent often feel fragile, and that breeds unhappiness.

Nurturing parents support activities that children undertake on their own. Lack of interest on a parent's part may be interpreted as a message that the activity is not valued.

Let your children experience the consequences of their decisions. This is one of life's best teachers; don't deprive them of the opportunity to learn in this way.

> ### It's Homework Time!
>
> *Studies show that if parents could enforce just one educational policy it should be this: Set aside a time for your child to do schoolwork — after school, after dinner, or whatever works for your child and the family. Obviously, this might vary from year to year, or from season to season, depending on extracurricular activities. During this time, there is no computer, no TV, no cell phone. It's homework time. And when homework is done, if the time isn't up, the child can read for pleasure.*

LISTENING

Listening is the most respectful thing one person can do for another. If you treat children with respect, they will be more likely to respect themselves. When parents have found the middle of the road, they will find themselves spending a lot of time listening to their children. (Experts suggest a good listener listens about 70 percent of the time and speaks only 30 percent of the time.)

Listen carefully to the child's problems, but be just as careful not to take responsibility for solving them.

JUDGING BEHAVIOR, NOT FEELINGS

Create good emotional intelligence by respecting your child's feelings.

Children need permission to feel their feelings so they can be aware of what they are dealing with and then let go of the negative thinking. At the same time, they shouldn't be allowed to use their feelings as an excuse for bad behavior. After all, parents still need to raise children who can function in a civilized manner. It's the child's behavior that should be judged, not his feelings.

Discipline needs to be administered clearly and decisively but not in a shaming or demeaning way. The parent must be honest, direct and clear. As you probably already know, children feel safer in an environment that provides healthy boundaries, where rules are clear and enforced, much the way rules are enforced at a baseball game.

Parents have to be especially careful with children who are simply not trying or who are demonstrating self-sabotaging behavior. Though these children may just want to protect themselves from feelings of despair, they need to understand they are only hurting themselves.

PROBLEM SOLVING

It is essential to promote problem-solving skills in children, especially those with learning differences. Giving advice too soon conveys the message, "You can't do it." Giving advice too often can make children feel incompetent. It also denies them the chance to solve a problem on their own.

Unsolicited advice is usually not heeded anyway. Even requested advice has to be very carefully given. Never assume that your advice will be used – or that it's even correct! Similarly, don't jump in and fix the problem.

Constructive encouragement *is* valuable. You could say, for example, "You've almost got it" or "I can see that you are working very hard at this; you're sticking to your study schedule." Allow the child to express feelings and frustrations. One of the best things you can do is to provide support for the effort.

Every time children succeed in figuring something out, they learn that they can figure out other things as well. That's a real gift to give.

Here's a hint on when you should problem solve: First, determine to whom a problem belongs. Whose needs are not being met? Who is losing time, money or energy? For example, if a child is having trouble with friends, it's the child's needs that are not being met. The problem belongs to the child. On the other hand, if a child misses a dental appointment and the parents are charged for it, the parents' needs have not been met.

If you focus your attention on situations that involve your needs only, you will go a long way toward empowering your child to handle his own problems.

DISCOVERING YOUR CHILD'S STRENGTHS

Most importantly, parents need to have a strong conviction that their children have real strengths and will find their path through life – even in the face of external evidence to the contrary, such as report cards, sneers, problems at home or work, or a child's negative self-assessment.

Jackie Stewart, the famous race car driver, recalled that his parents took pride in the way he ran the family gas station and in his ability to repair cars. They didn't focus on his poor schoolwork, even though they did what they could to help him by providing tutors and moral support. His parents also filled the shelves of the family home with his skeet-shooting trophies. Stewart went on to receive *Sports Illustrated* magazine's 1973 "Sportsman of the Year" award, the only auto racer to ever win the title.

Reread "Clue #6: Match Your Goals to Your Strengths" and apply it to your children. Observe what they like to do, what they find satisfying, and what they learn quickly. These are hints to identifying their talents and strengths.

A Self-Assessment For Parents

1. *Can you separate the concept of intelligence from academic abilities?*

2. *Can you reinforce effort as opposed to achievement?*

3. *Can you help your children develop a love of learning by reading aloud to them and making the discovery of knowledge an adventure?*

4. *Can you provide your children with an opportunity for real achievement and the development of social skills?*

5. *Can you teach your children that everyone has strengths and weaknesses by truly accepting your own limitations?*

6. *Can you encourage your children to set goals within their own control?*

7. *Can you accept the fact that life is difficult?*

8. *Can you make your children responsible for the consequences of their actions?*

9. *Can you make your children feel loved, cared for, and supported for who they are?*

GIVING RECORDED TEXT TO YOUR CHILD

Giving Recorded Text to Your Child

When is the right time to give recorded text to children?

I believe that as soon as children's reading ability lags behind their intellectual ability, they should be introduced to recorded books. (This is usually first identified around third or fourth grade.) This way, they won't be deprived of information that fuels their intellect and curiosity. Minds thrive on information.

Some professionals don't think it's wise to give recorded text to children at all. They believe that kids will stop trying to learn to read if they can listen to a book instead. But as a dyslexic reader, I know this isn't true. If I *could* have learned to read, I *would* have learned to read.

Still, it's important to evaluate each case individually to determine if it's wise to introduce recorded text.

Listening to recorded books is a wonderful tool for those with a reading disability; it opens worlds that are otherwise inaccessible. I didn't have the opportunity to listen to a book until I was in high school, when Denny's mother, Mildred, lent me set of vinyl records with performances of Shakespearean plays. I put one on my record player, and I was delighted. I couldn't have read those plays, but I wanted to. When I returned the set to Mildred, it was a worn-out mess.

Still, listening to a recorded book is more cumbersome and time-consuming than simply picking up a book from your night table and reading it. Maybe more importantly, reading to oneself allows the mind to enter a peaceful state, which doesn't happen as readily when you listen.

If you've decided to introduce your child to recorded text, it's best to start with entertaining material. You can purchase audiobooks from area bookstores or borrow them from your public library. Pick something that all the kids are reading, such as *Harry Potter*. By listening to the story, your child can take part in his peers' conversation and not be left out because the books are too hard to read.

You can instill in your children a love of reading before they can read on their own by snuggling up with them and reading a story aloud. That's how my mom nurtured my love of books. As kids get older and start to read on their own, you can still read to — and with — them. It's a special time, no matter what their age. At bedtime, you can give children a choice between turning out the light or reading for a little bit first. That's a great way to encourage reading!

Together with your child, create an inviting "listening/reading" corner with a comfortable chair or a stack of pillows. The player should sit out with the book beside it, along with pencils, highlighters, notepads, spare batteries and/or an AC outlet for recharging. The area should have a good reading light, along with anything else that would make it a special place for your child.

By putting together a reading corner, you will increase the amount of time your child spends "reading." The more a child listens and follows along in a book, the better his reading will become. It helps considerably to see what words look like in print.

Dyslexic readers must find their own way to best use recorded text. Parents need to honor their children's instincts and not force them to do it any one way.

While children might be reluctant to listen to recorded text in school, where doing so makes them feel different from their classmates, home might be a different story. But don't force them. In the privacy of your home, offer recorded text to your children; let them know it's available. Also let them know that the choice is theirs to make – not yours. "This is your life. You decide," you could say. Give them the problem *and* the chance to solve it.

I have a large wicker basket that holds my player, the book, headphones, highlighters, spare batteries, etc. I can carry it around the house. For travel, I use a backpack so I can take all of this with me. Recently, I've started taking my laptop, which is loaded with software that can read a book to me.

Almost There, Then a Rock Slide

"For a dyslexic who does not yet know he is dyslexic, life is like a big high wall you never think you will be able to climb or get over. The moment you understand there is something called dyslexia, and there are ways of getting around the problem, the whole world opens up."

- Jackie Stewart, nicknamed "The Flying Scot," three-time Formula One racing champion

ROUGH ROAD AHEAD

Rough Road Ahead

It's hard to wake up every morning ready to fight a half-dozen battles just to get your balance. It's exhausting. But that's what life is like for many people with learning disabilities.

Throughout my life, I've been told what I could not do:

• *I couldn't be a messenger in elementary school because I couldn't read.*

• *I wasn't college material.*

• *I couldn't get my master's degree because I didn't write well enough.*

• *I'd never get my doctorate because I wouldn't pass the statistics course.*

When it comes to problem solving, dyslexia has given me a lot of practice.

Attaining my doctorate after many, many years of hard work – and dealing with the frustration –wasn't the end of my challenges. First, I had to work 2,000 hours in a clinical setting under the supervision of a licensed psychologist. *That* wasn't a problem. It would take a couple of years.

But after that, I would have to sit for the licensing examination.

In preparation for the exam, it was recommended that people take a review course. It is not uncommon for intelligent, well-trained psychologists from fine universities to fail the exam the first time they take it. The competition is tough. The state will license only so many psychologists each year, and the number varies from state to state and from year to year.

Then I discovered how much reading was required for the review course. "Impossible!" I said aloud as it sank in. I had gotten this far, but I couldn't imagine how I was going to proceed. What if none of it was available on audiotape?

For the first time in my life, I thought that the rock slide across my path was impassable. It haunted me that night in a dream. I was going somewhere important in the darkness of night, and I had a sense of urgency and dread. Every time I thought I was approaching the destination, there would be an insurmountable obstacle in my way. No matter how far I backed up and how many other routes I took, I always wound up at the same place, blocked and frightened in the dark.

The review course material arrived in the mail. Stacked up, it was a foot and half high, maybe two. I knew I wouldn't be able to read all of it. And my fear was confirmed. There were no tapes, only written material.

Most people study the course materials for about six weeks and then take the exam, but I couldn't read that much in six weeks. Or two months. Or even a year.

I had gotten through my graduate work thanks in large part to Recording for the Blind & Dyslexic and by being willing to take one course at a time. But with this stack of impossible-for-me-to-read material, I was stymied.

Out of fear and frustration, I fell back into the ideas that people had imposed on me throughout my life. *I couldn't do it.*

In the past, I always knew I could find a way, but this time I couldn't see any possibility. However, I did have a vague sense of what I needed to do: *I needed to stay in action.* That had always been my salvation before – "keep on keepin' on"! I kept open to what might be out there to help me. I did not go into hiding.

When you stay open and active, the universe will provide.
When you close yourself off, that's when the real trouble begins.
When you are isolated, you are avoiding the issues that face you.

I called the company that gave the prep course to see if there was an audio version of the material. The call confirmed what I had heard – only written material, nothing else.

I asked everyone who crossed my path if they knew where I could get the review course material on tape. I kept putting my problem out there, in the hope that someone would have an idea, a friend, or a contact. An *anything*. I became more outgoing than I was comfortable with. I was looking for a needle in a haystack.

This continued for months, during which time I didn't do any studying. I tried to look at the material, but it was impossible for me to read and process in its printed form. I knew it would be a waste of time to try to read all that information. I read at a snail's pace.

Then something amazing happened. I called the prep course company again, this time to ask how long their material stayed current – I knew getting someone to record it for me would take months and months. Once again, I told the receptionist about my problem, as I did each time I called. But on this day, it wasn't the usual receptionist, and the woman who was filling in for her had a lead for me. She gave me the phone number of a blind man from the Midwest whose wife had been painstakingly recording all the course material for him on audiotape. *Exactly* what I needed!

I called. The man told me that his wife had been reading the material into a simple tape recorder, and they had already recorded a lot of the information. (He had been trying for years to pass the exam without success, which did not help my confidence.) Out of nothing but kindness, they made copies of all the tapes for me. It must have taken them days and days to do this. Then, they mailed 61 cassettes to me. When I received the tapes, I was filled with gratitude for these people who so generously helped me – and because I could finally study *my* way.

My mother-in-law, Mildred; one of my best friends, Marlene; and others volunteered to record the material that had not yet been read aloud. A retired physician recorded the medical sections for me.

Now that I had the tapes, I was able to clear my mind – and just as importantly, clear my desk and bookshelves to make room for the challenge to come.

Clutter is distracting for everyone, but especially for people with a learning disability. We need physical and mental space to work.

It was a beautiful fall day. The leaves were showing their first bit of color. As I was reorganizing the things on my desk, I paused and opened the window so I could smell the season. A breeze blew in. I picked up a book, and some papers that had been under it fluttered off my desk.

Then I heard a sound, a little click, followed by the sound of something rolling. Something had fallen off my desk and was rolling across the hardwood floor toward me. It stopped at my shoe. I leaned over and, with wide eyes, plucked it up between two fingers. There it was – my perfect, round, beautiful pearl.

It hadn't been lost forever after all. The pearl had been just sitting there on my desk, beneath papers and books, waiting for me to find it. I picked it up. It made me think about what a pearl goes through to become itself. Perhaps it was the same process I was going through.

CHAPTER 33

SCALING MOUNTAINS OF INFORMATION

Scaling Mountains
of Information

Even though I now had the tapes, I was still dealing with what appeared to be a mammoth job. It takes longer to listen than it takes a normal reader to read.

There was another huge problem: How could I keep this information in my head for up to a year and a half, which was the time it would take me to listen to the tapes? Shorter-term memory can hold information for hours or days or, at most, even months. That wasn't long enough for me.

I needed to find a way to boost my brain's ability to retain material over a longer time.

Here's what I did: I began to focus on the psychology of memory, which was, crazily enough, actually part of the course material. I was able to apply the material on how memory works to the process of preparing for the exam.

For example, the brain tends to have better recall of information from the beginning and end of a study session. If I were to read a list of 12 random numbers and ask you to repeat them, you'd have higher recall accuracy of the first and last numbers than of those in the middle of the list.

The same concept applies to studying. You tend to remember what you learn at the beginning and end, so I kept the sessions short.

To move information into long-term memory, one needs to overstudy it – five or six times beyond the time when you believe you've learned it.

- I created flash cards and looked at them four, five or six times after I had memorized them. The repetition reinforced the pathways. I marked the card each time I studied it.

- I used other good basic memory concepts, such as looking at the cards before I went to sleep.

- I always kept a pack of cards with me in my pocket or handbag, so whenever the opportunity presented itself – walking in the park, waiting to pick up the kids at school – I could review them.

- I memorized for short periods – 20 minutes. Even a quick five-minute session is worthwhile.

It seemed to be working. I stayed in action, and I was pacing myself. On weekends, I took a break from the more intense type of studying. I was fascinated by what I was learning. Psychology intrigued me, and my love for it helped see me through.

The Premack Principle of Reinforcement states that it's best to put tasks that are less pleasurable and less likely for you to do before those that are more pleasurable or more likely for you to do. I'd roll out of bed and study even before getting dressed. Then that task was out of the way and I could go about my day.

I kept my perspective. My family came first. I maintained strong rela-tionships with my friends. I kept myself physically fit. In the back of my mind I knew it was possible that I could fail, and so I couldn't risk everything for it. But I also knew I could pass. It might take me six times longer to study than it took someone else, but it was possible. In the end I would know the information as well as – if not better than – others.

To keep my perspective and pace myself, I set a study schedule.

- As I took the review course, I kept in mind a report that showed if you review your notes within 48 hours of class, then you will learn 80 percent more than students who don't review their notes.

- My brain works best in the morning, and so I made a note in my appointment planner to study then.

- I tackled the hardest things first while my mind was fresh.

- I listened to the tapes and created flash cards and charts.

- I rewarded myself with little stars in my planner when I completed a study session.

- I made sure to take plenty of breaks.

I didn't always follow my own study rules. One day, I felt anxious and studied way too much. That night, I again had the dream about the boulders in my path, but when I woke up and looked at all the stars in my planner, I felt really good: I was keeping my agreement with myself.

The end result was completely out of my control, but the *process* was totally within my control.

I promised myself that I would not even think about taking the exam until I had read through all of the material once and highlighted it. Because this took so long, the exam material would change, and I began to receive updates from the prep course company. That didn't help to simplify things.

There were so many topics to cover: general psychology, abnormal psych, lifespan development, social psych, statistics, assessment, etc. I was clear about the psychological concepts, but the words, especially the proper nouns, would get me stuck. I had to put them on charts, where they would be visually organized and logically associated with each other, so I could review them the night before the test. Dyslexics need many context clues to understand what they are learning.

I bought poster-sized sheets of graph paper and made huge maps of each subject area. These were simple charts, but they allowed me to record as much detail as I needed about every subject. I used a pencil so I could erase my mistakes. Today these are called **concept maps**.

We all learn via the five senses, but many dyslexic readers particularly benefit from seeing and doing — the kinesthetic experience. The act of creating concept maps and flash cards – drawing them and seeing them – is a very real part of learning. It may work for you, too.

After a year and a half of preparation, I was finally ready to take the exam. I put on my pearl necklace for good luck. When I walked into the testing center I was calm and confident – not that I would necessarily pass but that I had done every single thing within my ability to prepare. That went a long way.

I took the test. I was plenty nervous about the results. A few weeks later, an envelope from the state arrived. Did I mention that I was nervous?

I was thrilled with my score. Not the highest ever recorded, of course, but more than enough to qualify in Pennsylvania – or in any state. I did it! Someone had read the exam questions to me, but the only extra time I was given was to make up for the time it took him to read. That was the only accommodation I was given.

I had conquered the words I needed for the exam, but I didn't take on all the review material at once. I didn't lock myself up in a room and study until my eyes burned. I did exactly what I needed to do. In prepping for the exam, I took my time, paced myself and enjoyed the process.

You remember the rock slide dream I had when I first realized that taking the review course would be almost impossible? After I passed the exam, I had it again. It wasn't pleasant, but it wasn't terrifying this time. The rock slide was there in all its glory, but in this dream it wasn't the dark of night. It was daytime, and the light revealed something that was probably true the whole time: If I walked to the end of the rock pile, and if I didn't mind walking over some rough terrain clogged with high weeds, I could walk around the obstruction. Of course, in the dark this was impossible to see, but when the sun was shining, it was clear as day.

I got around that mess. I got around it *one word at a time.*

CHAPTER 34

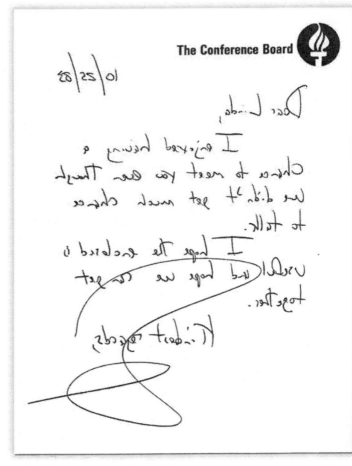

This letter was written to the author by
Delos Smith (Smitty), who even in adulthood
was still writing backward.

Epilogue:

What My Life Is Like Now

Life is not a matter of living happily ever after. It's not a movie or a TV show that ends in nice neat situations.

My dyslexia is no longer painful to me, nor do I want to be anyone other than who I am. I see my learning difference as just another part of me – like my brown eyes or my petite size. It's part of my humanness.

Today I am a working psychologist. I'm still passionate about the study of psychology and happily addicted to watching people change and succeed. I get to see light bulbs turn on in people's heads. When you love what you do, it's not work.

With time, I've come to recognize the treasures I've found along the road to managing my dyslexia. My verbal, problem-solving and conceptual thinking skills are all well-honed. I'm creative. I can see the big picture. I'm good at delegating, which is how I was able to write this book. I asked for help – and I got it!

"I have learned how to be different. After I learned to be different, I enjoyed being different. It is so much fun to walk to a different drummer." - Delos R. Smith, a global economist and a dyslexic reader

---

Dyslexia gets much easier as you get older. Without doubt, school is the most challenging time. But dyslexia doesn't go away.

I think dyslexia is a pain in the neck. Good creative ideas and well-thought-through points still get stuck in my head. The hardest part is finding a way to express them. My son Keith says that for him, dyslexia is a cosmetic problem. The words he communicates make sense out loud or in his head, but on the page or in an e-mail message they are not a pretty sight.

I wish I were a better writer and reader, but who doesn't wish they were better at some things?

When I read, you can still hear the dyslexia. There is no mistaking it. There is little fluidity. I get caught on a word and can't get past it.

When I was about 40, I realized for the first time in my life that I felt safe reading aloud. My family and I were at a Passover seder. Even though I knew I would have some trouble, I took my turn without trying to evade my fate. As I was reading, my little nephew – a grade-schooler himself – began giggling the way my classmates would have laughed three decades earlier. My sister-in-law shushed him. Now, in this safe environment, his giggling didn't hurt. But I did remember.

At times, I still get frustrated and angry when I repeatedly misdial a phone number or when the wrong word comes out of my mouth, even though I'm thinking of the right word. It bothers me when I can't rapidly recall the name of a person I met or a restaurant I visited. I get irritated at how long it can take me to do things that others do quickly.

But it passes. Often, I can laugh at the mistakes I make and the wrong words I use.

When I'm with a group of people, it can be tough to keep up with the cadence of the conversation. I'm still stymied by all that rapid naming and phoneme awareness. That's why Keith and I both do our best to avoid socializing in groups. We are much better one-on-one. At a wedding or party, I dance a lot.

I get nervous when I have to introduce people, but I'm not alone. A lot of people who don't have dyslexia are also afraid that they won't remember names.

Directions are challenging, too. Finding my way around a new place invariably takes me longer than it takes my companions.

At restaurants, I can read the menu, but one word will get past me and I'll end up with an entrée I don't want. So I ask others what they are going to eat, and I always ask to order last. I'll listen to the waiter recite the specials and order one of those, or just tell the waiter what I'd like to eat and see if the kitchen can make it. This works extremely well.

It is difficult to understand my brain. Easy things are hard and hard things present no problem. Learning to read is difficult; learning the higher levels of doctoral statistics is less demanding for me.

"Over time, reading performances improve in both good readers and poor readers. However the gap between the two groups remain."
- Sally Shaywitz, author of Overcoming Dyslexia: A New and Complete Science-Based Program for Reading Problems at Any Level

---

Learning a new language feels nearly impossible – it took me so long to learn English. If I had to learn a new language, I would have to keep remembering that, like English, other languages are finite. But for now, I'm just glad I don't have to tackle a foreign language.

When I don't appear too bright to the outside world, I don't take it seriously. I remind myself that "I know I'm fine and so are you." Sometimes it's fun to use humor. I take on the personality of a ditzy broad.

One of the most comforting things I learned in my studies to be a psychologist is this: The most attractive people are competent people *who make mistakes.* That's great, because I certainly make plenty of mistakes!

My reading ability has improved ever so slowly, but it has improved. I now read *USA Today* articles. I am just beginning to read short books. Before I go to sleep, I read a handful of pages to myself – one, two, three, four – and I love it.

Don't think for one minute that I am suggesting it's pleasant to have a learning difference in a literate society. However, working your way through the challenges, even though they may be frustrating and exhausting, can take you to a place of satisfaction and fulfillment far beyond what you could have hoped for or imagined. I chose education as my path, and it has brought me challenges, success and a lot of joy.

The Flight of a Bumblebee

Take a moment to picture a bumblebee. You are probably remembering that it has a fat black and yellow body. If you keep remembering, you'll see its thin little wings. It doesn't look like it should be able to fly. But no one told this to the bee.

Further education might not be your path, but there are many routes. In truth, life's possibilities are endless, even if you have a learning difference, and in some ways, *especially* if you have a learning difference – because you'll learn to think outside the box. That's why British billionaire Richard Branson, who has dyslexia, made a different kind of airline – Virgin Atlantic. The late neuropsychiatrist Dr. Richard Wyatt, who also had dyslexia, attributed his groundbreaking research on schizophrenia to his ability to solve problems in a non-traditional way.

People told me that I couldn't go to college. They told me I couldn't get a master's degree and a Ph.D. They told me I couldn't write a book. I told myself I couldn't write a book.

Luckily, I didn't listen. Three years later, you're turning the pages of my book. Its existence is beyond my wildest dreams.

As a child, I sensed the magic of books. Although my severe dyslexia prevented me from reading, I yearned to read books. Somehow, I knew that the right book at the right time could be pure magic – an opening of the universe. Now that I can read or listen to a book, I've discovered that I was right: Reading a book can change your life, and no one should miss what books have to offer.

My dream is that *One Word at a Time* will be meaningful to you. May it open for you the splendid world of books – and exciting possibilities.

With love, respect and wishes for you to have everything you wish for yourself.

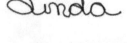

Linda Greenbaum Tessler, Ph.D.

Your Packing List for Your Trip

❏ A working understanding of your learning disability.

❏ Your emotional intelligence. Don't worry: you can pick up a lot more along the way.

❏ A healthy dose of curiosity and self-motivation.

❏ The ideas in this book that have inspired you to take action. Refer to the notes you made on pages 18-19.

❏ The Six Clues to Successfully Managing a Learning Disability. Refer back to them if you get stuck.

> ❏ Take Action
>
> ❏ Prioritize and Pace Yourself
>
> ❏ Set up a Two-Tiered Support System (technical and social)
>
> ❏ Look Inside and Like What You See
>
> ❏ Create Balance
>
> ❏ Match Your Strengths to Your Goals

Giving Credit Where Credit Is Due

Words do not come easily to dyslexics. All my life, I have memorized the phrases and expressions of others in order to express myself. Likewise, I've borrowed many of the words and phrases in this book. All my mentors, writers, and the others who have come before me deserve recognition. I have given everybody credit as best as I can recall. If I have inadvertently missed anyone, I apologize.

Bibliography

Bandler, R. (1985). *Using Your Brain – For a Change*. Maob, UT: Real People Press.

Badian, Nathlie A. (1997). *Annals of Dyslexia*, Vol. 47: "Dyslexia and the Double Deficit Hypothesis." Maryland: The International Dyslexia Association.

Bloom, B. S. (editor) (1985). *Developing Talent in Young People*. New York: Ballantine Books.

Bourne, Edmund (1995). *The Anxiety and Phobia Workbook*. Oakland, CA: New Harbinger Publications, Inc.

Brabham, D. (January/February 2004). *Psychology Today*: "Is Your Head Tripping You Up?" p. 61-64.

Brutten, M., Richardson, S. O., & Mangel, C. (1973). *Something's Wrong With My Child: A Parents' Book About Children With Learning Disabilities*. New York: Harcourt Brace Jovanovich, Inc.

Buchman, Dana with Farber, Charlotte (2006). *A Special Education: One Family's Journey Through the Maze of Learning Disabilities*. Cambridge, MA: Da Capo Press.

Buckingham, Marcus and Clifton, Donald Ph.D. (2001). *Now, Discover Your Strengths*. New York: Simon and Schuster.

Burns, David (1980). *Feeling Good: The New Mood Therapy*. New York: Penguin Books USA Inc.

Carter, Jay (2003). *Nasty People: How to Stop Being Hurt by Them Without Stooping to Their Level* (revised edition). New York, NY: McGraw-Hill.

Clarke, Louise (1973). *Can't Read, Can't Write, Can't Talk Too Good Either*. United States: Penguin Books.

Covey, S. R. (1990). *The 7 Habits of Highly Effective People: Powerful Lessons in Personal Change*. New York: Fireside.

Doskoch, P. (November/December 2005). *Psychology Today*: "The Winning Edge." Vol. 38, No. 6, p. 42-52.

Erikson, E. H. (1963, second ed.). *Childhood and Society*. New York: W. W. Norton & Company.

Evans, P. (1992). *The Verbally Abusive Relationship: How to Recognize It and How to Respond*. Holbrook, MA: Adams Media Corporation.

Faber, A., & Mazlish, E. (1980). *How to Talk So Kids Will Listen & Listen So Kids Will Talk*. New York: Avon Books, Inc.

Ford, Anne with John-Richard Thompson and Mel Levine (2004). *Laughing Allegra: The Inspiring Story of a Mother's Struggle and Triumph Raising a Daughter with Learning Disabilities*. New York: Newmarket Press.

Ford, Anne with John-Richard Thompson (2007). *On Their Own: Creating an Independent Future for Your Adult Child with Learning Disabilities and ADHD: A Family Guide*. New York: Newmarket Press.

Frankl, V. E. (1959). *Man's Search for Meaning: An Introduction to Logotherapy*. New York: A Touchstone Book.

Gardner, Howard (June 1984). *Psychology Today:* "The Seven Frames of Mind." Vol. 18, No. 6, p. 20-26.

Goleman, D. (1995). *Emotional Intelligence: Why It Can Matter More Than IQ* (an audiobook). Los Angeles: Audio Renaissance Tapes.

Goleman, D. (1998). *Working With Emotional Intelligence* (an audiobook). Los Angeles: Audio Renaissance.

Gordon, T. (1970). *P.E.T. Parent Effectiveness Training: The Tested New Way to Raise Responsible Children*. New York: Peter H. Wyden, Inc.

Grubin, David (2001). PBS Home Video: *The Secret Life of the Brain*. New York: Thirteen/WNET.

Hallowell, E. M., & Ratey, J. J. (1994). *Driven to Distraction: Recognizing and Coping With Attention Deficit Disorder from Childhood Through Adulthood*. New York: Pantheon Books.

Isaacson, Walter (2008). *Einstein: His Life and His Universe*. New York: Simon & Schuster.

Kantrowitz, Barbara and Anne Underwood (Nov. 22, 1999). *Newsweek Magazine:* "Dyslexia and the New Science of Reading."

LDA Newsbriefs (May/June 2006) "Types of Learning Disabilities." Pittsburgh, PA.: An Official Publication of the Learning Disabilities Association of America. Vol. 41, No. 3.

Learning Disabilities Association of America (2001). "Signs and Symptoms of Dyslexia." Excerpted from the LDA of California and UC Davis M.I.N.D. Institute "Q.U.I.L.T.S." Calendar 2001-2002.

Learning Disabilities Association of America (2004). "Symptoms of Learning Disabilities." Pittsburgh, PA.

Lerner, H. G. (1985). *The Dance of Anger: A Woman's Guide to Changing the Patterns of Intimate Relationships*. New York: Harper & Row.

Levine, M. (2002). *A Mind at a Time: America's Top Learning Expert Shows How Every Child Can Succeed* (an audiobook). New York: Simon & Schuster Audio Division.

Levine, M. (1990). *Keeping Ahead in School: A Student's Book About Learning Abilities and Learning Disorders*. Cambridge, MA: Educators Publishing Service, Inc.

Levine, M. (March 2003). Referenced Philip Lieberman in a speech on Learning Disabilities. Union League, Philadelphia, PA.

Levine, M. (2003). *The Myth of Laziness: America's Top Learning Expert Shows How Kids —and Parents – Can Become More Productive*. New York: Simon & Schuster.

Lieberman, Philip. (1984). *The Biology and Evolution of Language*. Cambridge, MA: Harvard University Press.

Lions Clubs International & Quest International (1985). The *Surprising Years: Understanding Your Changing Adolescent – a Book for Parents*. Granville, OH: Quest International.

Marano, H. E. (November/December 2004). *Psychology Today*, "A Nation of Wimps," Vol. 37, No. 6, p. 58-70, 103.

McGowan, K. (March/April 2006). *Psychology Today*, "The Hidden Side of Happiness," Vol. 39, No. 2, p. 68-78.

McGraw, P.C. (2001). *Self Matters: Creating Your Life From the Inside Out*. New York: Free Press.

Michaelson, Peter. (1999). *Freedom from Self-Sabotage: The Intelligent Reader's Guide to Success and Self-Fulfillment*. Santa Fe, NM: Prospect Books.

Midwest Center for Stress and Anxiety, Inc. (1985). *Attacking Anxiety and Depression: A Self-Help, Self-Awareness Program for Stress, Anxiety and Depression*. Oak Harbor, OH: Midwest Center for Stress and Anxiety, Inc.

Monk Kidd, Sue (2002). *The Secret Life of Bees*. New York, NY: Viking Penguin.

Nosek, K. (1997). *Dyslexia in Adults: Taking Charge of Your Life*. Dallas, TX: Taylor Publishing Company.

Osman, B. B., & Blinder, H. (1982). *No One to Play With: The Social Side of Learning Disabilities*. New York: Random House.

Peck, M. S. (1978). *The Road Less Traveled: A New Psychology of Love, Traditional Values and Spiritual Growth*. New York: A Touchstone Book.

Pelham, Brett. (Spring 2000). "Emotional Intelligence: A Seminar for Health Professionals." Mind Matters Seminars, Mountain View, CA.

Rathvon, N. (1996). *The Unmotivated Child: Helping Your Underachiever Become a Successful Student*. New York: Fireside.

Robbins, A. (1986). *Unlimited Power*. New York: Fawcett Columbine.

Ruiz, D. M. (1999). *The Four Agreements: a Toltec Wisdom Audio Book*. San Rafael, CA: Amber-Allen Publishing.

Shaywitz, Sally. (2003). *Overcoming Dyslexia: A New and Complete Science-Based Program for Reading Problems at Any Level*. New York: Alfred A. Knopf.

Silberman, M. L., & Wheelan, S. A. (1980). *How to Discipline Without Feeling Guilty: Assertive Relationships With Children*. New York: Hawthorn Books.

Simpson, E. (1979). *Reversals: A Personal Account of Victory Over Dyslexia*. Boston: Houghton Mifflin Company.

Taylor, James. (1997) *Hourglass*, "Enough To Be On Your Way." Columbia.

Tessler, L. G. (1987). *Descriptions of Characteristics and Coping Strategies of Nine Famous Self-Perceived Dyslexics*. Ann Arbor, MI: UMI.

West, T. G. (1997). *In the Mind's Eye: Visual Thinkers, Gifted People With Dyslexia and Other Learning Difficulties, Computer Images and the Ironies of Creativity*. Amherst, NY: Prometheus Books.

Wolf, M. & Bowers, P. (2000). *Journal of Learning Disabilities*, "The Question of Naming-Speed Deficits in Developmental Reading Disability: An Introduction to the Double-Deficit Hypothesis. Vol. 33, p. 322-324.

More Praise for
One Word at a Time

"*One Word at a Time* is a concise, easy-to-use handbook for people with dyslexia and their families and friends. Linda Tessler uses her own experiences to personalize the information, which covers not only some of the basics but also the sometimes-emotional challenge of living with dyslexia. It's a great book for anyone who wants to learn more about dyslexia. Linda makes the book accessible to everyone. It's something I can share with my daughter as she learns to live with dyslexia and realizes that it only adds to the richness of life."

— Hunt Lowry, CEO/President of Roserock Entertainment and producer of many box office hits, such as A Time to Kill and Last of the Mohicans. Hunt is the recipient of the IDA's Pinnacle Award, which recognizes a dyslexic individual who has made significant achievements in his field and is a role model for others with dyslexia.

"Sensitive and informative, *One Word at a Time* offers advice and strategies so that those with dyslexia can achieve success. It will be a great resource for our students, who will enjoy the author's life experience with dyslexia – and her successes. We will add the book to our Learning Cognition classes. It's an easy read that's suitable for all ages."

— Richard G. Collins, Ph.D., Executive Director, Brehm Preparatory School & OPTIONS Program at Brehm

"*One Word at a Time* offers hope, encouragement, and superb practical advice for those of us (teachers, parents, and particularly individuals) who have lived with LD. The information and accompanying anecdotes are clear, cleverly presented, and extremely practical."

— Margie Gillis, Ed.D., Project Director, Haskins Literacy Initiative, which is affiliated with Yale University

"*One Word at a Time* recounts the inspiring life journey of a dyslexic reader – from secrecy and embarrassment to confidence and independence. Writing autobiographically in a conversational style, Linda Tessler posits a proactive, self-assuring message for parents, coupled with practical strategies for dyslexic children and adults. She has given back to the LD community by sharing her struggles, triumphs and wisdom while focusing parents on validating feelings, developing strategies for vulnerabilities, and trusting their innate judgment of their child. I recommend this book for Center School parents."

– Joseph T. Devlin, Head of School, Center School, Abington, PA

"*One Word at a Time* challenges each of us to recognize, understand and appreciate dyslexia and the related issues. Linda has told a personal story of courage and hope that individuals with dyslexia, their family members and educators need to hear. You will feel as if the author is speaking directly to you as she shares not only her experiences but also the lessons she learned. The book represents a spectacular accomplishment for her but more than that it will be an invaluable resource for the reader. Thank you, Linda."

– Nancy Hennessey, M.Ed., a teacher, administrator, diagnostician and consultant in both regular and special education, is Immediate Past President of the International Dyslexia Association

"*One Word at a Time* provides information, inspiration and great insight into the struggles caused by a learning disability. I am excited that there is an easy-to-read book for parents, students and professionals about the challenges of dyslexia and other language-based learning disabilities. These students and their parents are on a lifelong journey, and this book is a great compass for them to use as they travel through each new stage."

– Pat Roberts, Executive Director of the Academy in Manayunk, which opened in conjunction with The Lab School of Washington®